BUILDINGS IN MINIATURE

BUILDINGS
IN MINIATURE

GERALD E. JENSEN

Photographs by Jack Jensen

CHILTON BOOK COMPANY
RADNOR, PENNSYLVANIA

This book is lovingly dedicated to my mother, Hilary,
for giving me the gift of life

Contents

Acknowledgments

A special thanks to all the many people who helped to make this book possible. To my son, Jack, for the many hours of time required for the photography. To my wife, Jeanne, for her support and understanding during the trying times. To all my children, who helped in more ways than they know, my thanks.

INTRODUCTION

History indicates that miniatures first appeared in the sixteenth century when a European nobleman commissioned craftsmen to build miniature replicas for his daughter. That first dollhouse was commissioned by the Duke of Bavaria in 1558. Down through the centuries, craftsmen have devoted their time and effort to generate legacies by their precise attention to the smallest detail.

One of the prime examples of this is Queen Mary of England's Dollhouse, considered by many to be the best dollhouse in the world. This remarkable house was built as a gift for the Queen in the 1920s. The miniatures contained in this elaborate citadel are the products of dedicated craftspeople who spent endless hours creating artistic works that have become a legend in their own time. The meticulous detail of every piece of furniture and each individual accessory makes the entire dollhouse an outstanding work of art.

The leather-bound original volumes in the library were handwritten by the leading English writers of that time; there are hot and cold operating water faucets and original oil portraits of past English monarchs. The precision needed to produce a miniature operating vacumn cleaner requires a professional approach. The perfectly scaled and operating piano in the drawing room is another prime example of the prodigious craftsmanship that was required to produce these miniatures. All of this fine work was done in exquisite beauty befitting a Queen.

Prior to the building of this monument, a standardized scale in the miniature world did not exist. The scale that any craftsperson worked to was an individual decision. The publicity that this royal treasure received around the world was very instrumental in establishing the $\frac{1}{12}$ scale as the international standard.

There are many interesting museums on this side of the Atlantic which have acquired remarkable collections of miniatures, also. One of the more notable collections is the Thorn Room collection in the Phoenix Art Museum. It contains 16 rooms of English, French, Italian and American Period Furniture, all done in exquisite detail. Another Thorn Room Collection can be found in the Art Institute of Chicago. This is another finely detailed collection, and larger, being comprised of 68 miniature rooms of furniture depicting American, English and French interior decor.

The Thorn Rooms were designed and commissioned by Mrs. James Ward Thorn in the 1920's. Every construction detail of each room and each piece of furniture was done under the watchful eye of Mrs. Thorn. Her sole purpose in generating this display was that of preserving the historical significance of American and European interior decor.

The Science Museum of Chicago proudly displays the popular palace of actress Colleen Moore, which is nine feet square at the base and contains over 1000 pieces of miniature furniture and accessories. It is one of the few large-scale miniature castles in existence which has a room for a chapel built into the basic structure. Another highlight of this castle is the drawing room, which displays a chandelier built with diamonds, emeralds and pearls. The walls of this drawing room are painted with murals that portray the story of Cinderella.

The Mott's Collection located at the Knotts' Berry Farm in California is comprised of six antique houses and 35 shops containing over 150,000 miniature items. This collection required 66 years of collecting and building miniatures to attain its vast size.

The display of the Washington Doll's House and Toy Museum, located in Washington, D. C., contains the dollhouse of President Harrison's daughter, in addition to the Mexican Mansion, which was obtained from an antique store in Pueblo, Mexico. It stands seven feet tall and six feet wide. The exact date of origin has not been established in some thirty years of research. The Paige automobile and the vintage of the radio receiving tower indicate some of the work at least was done in the early 1920's. It is claimed to be the first and only Latin American miniature mansion in existence.

The Museum of History and Technology located at the Smithsonian Institute in Washington, D.C., contains the Faith Bradford Dollhouse, which was built in the early part of the 1900's. It is an impressive 22-room dollhouse, and contains many one-of-a-kind miniature treasures which are viewed by a countless number of people every day of the year.

Nostalgic influence and the desire to preserve historical monuments have overflowed into the miniature world and have been strong motivations in the construction of many miniature houses. Many people find miniatures to be a way to recapture the past. The foremost of the historical structures is a miniature White House, built by Jan and John Zweifel. The time required for the painstaking research and the actual building of this structure was over twenty years. This miniature structure is intended to be a replica of the White House as it existed on July 4, 1976. This ambitious project was built as a Bicentennial tribute to American independence. It was scheduled to tour the United States for two years and then be placed in the Smithsonian Institute in Washington, D. C.

The fascination of miniatures has intrigued a countless number of people, of every decade, for centuries. Displays of miniatures, whether in museums, art galleries or shopping centers, possess a magnetic force which attracts people of all ages to witness history being preserved in miniature.

Each year more and more admirers are added to the list of craftspeople devoted to expanding the realm of miniatures for self-enrichment and the enjoyment of countless other people. Modern day miniature houses have transcended the era of the cardboard boxes of the 1930's and the metal dollhouses of the 40's, to the magnificent wooden structures of the 1970's and 80's. The ever-increasing interest and demand for quality has transformed the once docile pasttime of little girls into the active realm of the adult world.

The fascination of the miniature world spans all walks of life, including doctors, lawyers, teachers, mailcarriers, housewives, engineers, secretaries, plumbers and businesspeople, and encompasses all age groups from senior citzens to teenagers. Building and collecting miniatures has become the fastest growing hobby in the United States today.

1
Building Materials

Wood

The lumber most commonly used for building the basic dollhouse structure is plywood, usually in 1/4, 3/8 or 1/2-inch thicknesses. My preference is for the 3/8-inch stock, because it is 25 percent lighter than the 1/2-inch plywood. The 1/4-inch material, while being quite a bit lighter in weight (33 percent), is not quite sturdy enough for me, and presents some problems when attempting to nail and glue the narrow edges. If plywood is to be utilized for most of the construction details, obtain the best possible grade to assure a good finished appearance.

Plywood panels are readily available from lumber yards and remodeling centers in sheets 4 feet wide by 8 feet long. Hardware stores, hobby stores and lumber yards will often have either 2-by-4-foot or 4-by-4-foot panels. If your workshop space is not sufficient to handle the full-size panel, purchase the smaller sizes or have the lumber dealer cut the larger panel to a manageable size. There generally is a nominal fee for this service.

Plywood

Cabinet grade plywood is the best plywood available. It is available with the surface layer made from birch, fir, oak and some pine. It is generally available in 1/4- and 1/2-inch thicknesses and is sometimes difficult to obtain in the 3/8-inch thickness. It is more expensive than other grades of plywood, but should be seriously considered if the exterior of the miniature house is to be left unfinished. It is available at custom cabinet shops and specialty lumber stores.

An A-A grade designation for plywood indicates that both surfaces are of Grade A quality. This grade of plywood may also be difficult to obtain

Fig. 1–1   Top to bottom: Chipboard; particle board; Grade A-A plywood; cabinet grade plywood

in some areas. It is generally available at custom cabinet shops and specialty lumber yards. It is slightly more expensive than more commonly available grades of plywood, such as A-B or A-C, but it is much easier to work with.

The next grade of plywood (A-B) has only one side of Grade A quality. The other side, designated as B Grade, may have some exposed knots. While this grade is completely acceptable for dollhouse construction, the presence of the exposed knots will detract from the appearance of the house unless the exterior is finished with clapboard siding, batten strips or stucco. Remember when cutting the individual parts for the house to have the imperfect side to the exterior so that it can be covered. This plywood is available at specialty lumber shops and the better lumber yards.

The least desirable grade is A-C. One side, designated as A, is of good quality; but the other side, designated as C quality, can contain some cracks, splits and knot holes that are not plugged. This grade, however, can also be used if the exterior is going to be covered with siding, to conceal the imperfections. This plywood is quite suitable for roof sections that will be covered with shingles. This grade is readily available and is the least expensive of the various grades of plywood. It is sometimes listed as Shop Grade, exterior.

Construction grades of plywood (C-D and C-X) contain rough surfaces and many imperfections and are not recommended for miniature house construction. They are mentioned so that the miniature builder will know what to avoid.

Particle Board

Particle board is a dense material (about twice the weight of plywood in the same thickness), but it is suitable for some construction features. The panels are fabricated in 4-by-8-foot sheets composed of sawdust, small wood chips and a resin binder. It cannot easily be nailed without chipping the edges, but predrilling holes for the nails will prevent this. Because it is so dense, it has a tendency to dull the saw blade rather quickly.

The surface of the board has a fairly rough texture that resembles stucco when painted. Another advantage is that it is easily glued to plywood and other materials. When used in conjunction with plywood, it can be nailed if the holes are predrilled. Joints should also be glued. Predrilled holes are also required when attaching hinges with screws. It is available at most lumber yards and remodeling centers and is inexpensive (about one third the cost of comparably sized plywood).

Chip Board

Chip board is similar to particle board in that it is composed of sawdust and large wood chips which are glued together to form 4-by-8-foot panels. It is about the same weight as plywood, and costs about half as much. It is a suitable material for covered roofs on the miniature house, or for other structures where a smooth surface is not an absolute necessity. Chip board is available at all lumber yards and remodeling centers and some hardware stores.

Finishes

Paints

Most specialty miniature shops and the better hobby and craft stores maintain a wide selection of quality paints designed specifically for the miniature house builder. These are generally quick drying, and are available in a large range of colors. The quick drying type is preferred by miniature builders because a second coat can generally be applied within one-half hour after the first coat.

The paints used for the exterior and trim can be high gloss, semi-gloss or matte finish, while the interior colors are usually of the matte finish.

Paint with a very short drying time can be obtained in spray cans, which allows the application of an even coat in the recesses of the small spindles found on porch and balcony railings. These paints are available in a full range of colors and in assorted sizes at most hardware stores and some hobby and miniature shops.

There are also many kinds of specialty paints available for miniature enthusiasts. Acrylic, oil-base and watercolor artists' paints can be used to personalize accessories and furniture pieces, as well as for decorating highlights on the house itself.

Another specialty paint is glass stain paint. This paint was designed to paint glass to simulate stained glass windows and does not have to be fired. It can also be used on smaller items like miniature bud vases and lamps. A person is restricted only by her/his imagination.

As another source of paint, check the local paint stores or the paint section of any large department store. In many cases they have quantities of paint mixed to the wrong color or that were returned by a customer. These mistakes can be excellent buys. For a small fee they will often change the shade for you, and it will still be a bargain. Also, sand paints or textured paints are often on sale; these are very suitable for a stucco effect on the house exterior.

Stains

Stains of various shades are available in water-base, vinyl-base and oil-base in liquid form. The oil-base produces the most satisfactory results and can be applied with a paint sponge, a cloth or a paint brush. Stain can be used on many different features, such as paneled walls, floors, staircases, picture frames and shingles.

The stains are available in small one-ounce jars, which are specifically designed for the miniature builder. The most desired colors are walnut, cherry, maple and mahogany.

When staining shingles, use a very dark color to accentuate the color contrast between the house color, the trim and the shingles. To obtain a shaded weathered look, use the spray can type of stain. The edges can be darkened with a second coat.

When staining small hardwood spindles, a second coat may be required to obtain an even finish. The tight grain of the hardwood does not absorb the stain as readily as softwoods do.

When staining staircases, wainscoting and railings, try to maintain a medium to a darker shade to blend with the color of the floors and door and window trim. Light-colored stains tend to blend the staircase into the surrounding background.

Varnish and Shellac

The final finishes, or varnish, can be obtained in a high gloss, semi-gloss (or satin) and matte finish in both liquid and spray-can form. The high gloss can be used on floors, staircases, and window and door casings, if a bright shine is desired. However, the more subdued satin finish is often preferred for all the miniature house components, as well as for finishing the furniture.

Another high gloss finish can be obtained with shellac. This finish can be reduced to a somewhat satin finish by adding denatured alcohol to the shellac at a one-to-one ratio. Care must be exercised when applying shellac with a brush, or surface bubbles will occur. Applying shellac in one direction only will minimize this condition.

2
TOOLS

Power Tools

Probably the most significant limiting factor of well-built miniature houses and furniture will be the type of tools that are available to the builder. It is true that a good carpenter can construct a well-built house using only a hammer, a framing square and a reliable handsaw. But if you are fortunate enough to possess or have access to more advanced tools, there isn't any feature that cannot be built from scratch.

The following section describes the tools that were utilized to construct the various projects contained in this book. The actual tools that you will employ will be determined by what is available to you and how much minute detail you actually want to build, rather than purchasing the finished item. If time is an important element, it may be prudent to purchase the required building components, either in the ready-cut form or the ready-made, assembled units. When buying tools, always buy the highest quality you can afford. With proper care, tools should last for many years.

Table Saw

Because of their limited table-top area, the smaller table saws cannot adequately handle the large panels of plywood required for the construction of most miniature dollhouses. A saw with an 8-inch diameter blade or larger is recommended for cutting of the large, 4-by-8-foot sheets of plywood, chip board and particle board. The smaller table saws, with the 4- to 6-inch blade, are suitable for the fine cutting required on the smaller dollhouse components.

Fig. 2–1   Dremel table saw (photo courtesy of Dremel Mfg.)

The Dremel table saw shown in Fig. 2–1 is an ideal choice for the smaller work. It contains a 4-inch blade which will cut up to a one-inch board at 90 degrees and up to a ¾-inch board at 45 degrees. For a smooth cut, select a fine-tooth blade.

The larger saws also use a fine-tooth sawblade to obtain a smooth cut. The plywood and veneer cutting sawblade will leave an edge which requires very little, if any, sanding. Utilize the table saw not only for straight cuts, but also for bevel cuts (Fig. 2–2), compound cuts, and miter cuts (Fig. 2–3). If dado cuts are going to be used, a dado blade will also be required.

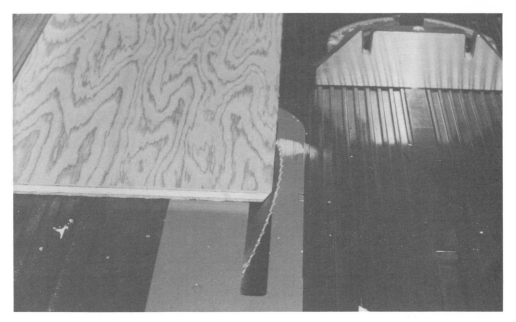

Fig. 2–2   Bevel cut with table saw

Fig. 2–3   Miter cut with table saw

Radial Saw

The radial saw will perform all the required functions of a saw, but it also can be utilized as a router for making trim molding by using the Jacob's chuck on the accessory end spindle of the motor shaft (Fig. 2–4). This ability makes the radial saw a more versatile piece of equipment. The standard table saw cannot be converted to accommodate router bits or other radial saw accessories.

A note of caution: when using the accessory end of the motor shaft, (1) remove the sawblade to prevent accidents, (2) determine the rotational direction of the shaft and feed material *only* into this rotation. Normally the rotation will be clockwise when using the accessory end. This will require feeding the strips of lumber from *left to right*. To obtain the best finished appearance, make two or more passes with the strips of lumber. On the first pass set the router bit height to obtain about one half to two thirds of the required cut depth. Then on the second pass, adjust the height of the router bit to obtain the desired cut. Making two cuts takes a little more time, but the end results are definitely worth the additional effort. Trying to obtain the desired molding configuration in only one pass usually causes excessive chipping and splitting of the wood by trying to remove too much material at one time.

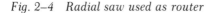

Fig. 2–4   Radial saw used as router

Feed the material into the router bit at a slow and constant speed to produce the best results. Feeding the material too fast or at an inconsistent speed will cause chatter and produce a rough finish on the molding. You can determine the proper rate of feed by the motor noise. When the lumber is fed at the proper speed, it will produce a smoothly running motor without chatter. If a chatter is produced, either the cut is too deep or the feed is too fast.

To avoid the dangers inherent in small pieces, cut the strip of lumber twice as wide as required and then contour *both* edges. Using the table saw or radial saw, cut the strip of lumber to the desired width.

Sabre Saw

The sabre saw (Fig. 2–5) is preferred for cutting openings in the walls for the doors and windows, and cutouts for the stairwells and arches. The hand-held keyhole saw will work almost as well, but it will require a larger size starting hole. Use a fine-tooth sawblade for a smooth finish. Some sabre saws are equipped with a variable speed control, which permits regulating the speed on any cutting operation. This feature is es-

Fig. 2–5   Sabre saw and electric drill

pecially useful when working with various thicknesses of material to obtain the proper speed and thus reduce the amount of edge splintering.

Electric Drill

The electric drill can be a standard ¼-inch diameter shank or larger. It is used primarily for drilling the ⅜-inch starter holes for the sabre saw-blade. It is also very useful for making dowel joints and drilling the pilot holes for wood screws.

Router

The router (Fig. 2–6) will permit you to make a larger amount of the specialty wood trim that is required for most dollhouses, if you prefer doing it yourself rather than purchasing the ready-made moldings. Various cutter bits allow you to make a variety of cove, bead and other specially shaped moldings. The standard ³/₁₆-inch router bits are generally the smallest size available at most hardware stores. Dremel produces the smaller ³/₃₂- and ³/₁₆-inch bead and cove cutting bits, which are available at most hobby and craft stores and at some hardware stores. The Dremel Moto-Tool has a router attachment available so it can be utilized as a hand-held router (Fig. 2–7), making the Moto-Tool a versatile piece of equipment. These are available at most hobby and hardware stores.

Lathe

The wood lathe can be used for making turned spindles such as the pillars on a porch or balcony, the ballisters for a staircase and the spindles for any railing. Lathes are available at most hardware stores, along with the required gouges. The Dremel Moto-Lathe (Fig. 2–8) is very suitable for the small spindle turnings that are used in both dollhouses and furniture. The Moto-Lathe and the associated small gouges are available at most hobby stores and hardware stores.

Electric Belt Sander

Electric belt sanders are available in sizes from the large commercial type to the smaller hobby size. Because of the limited amount of sanding required during the construction of a dollhouse, a smaller unit will suffice. The electric sander is very useful for dressing the edge of plywood pieces to remove any splinters that may be present.

The Dremel belt sander (Fig. 2–9) has a disc sanding portion which is especially useful for sanding the edges of rough-cut plywood. The belt section is useful when working with contour shaped pieces. There are various sizes of grit sanding paper available for the sander, from the coarse grit to the very fine. The belt sander, like the rest of the Dremel

Fig. 2–6
Router

Fig. 2–7
Dremel Moto-Tool with
router attachment
(photo courtesy of
Dremel Mfg.)

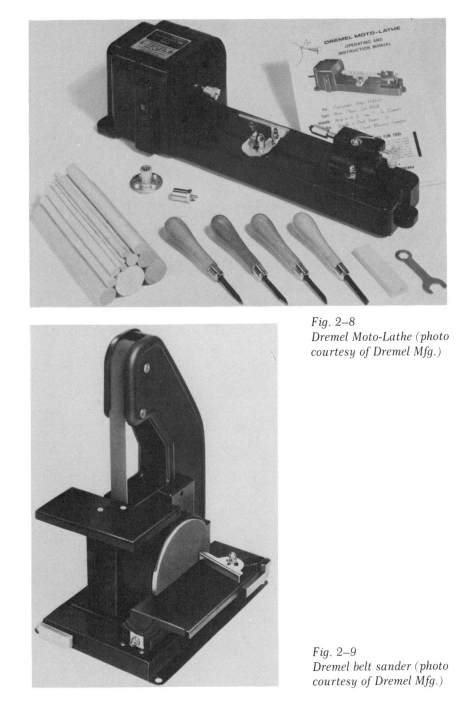

Fig. 2–8
Dremel Moto-Lathe (photo
courtesy of Dremel Mfg.)

Fig. 2–9
Dremel belt sander (photo
courtesy of Dremel Mfg.)

line, is a compact unit and requires very little space for storage, which is another desirable feature if workspace is limited.

Jigsaw

The jigsaw is a versatile tool and highly recommended. It is ideal for cutting pieces of irregular shapes, like eave brackets or roof supports on a Victorian-style house. It is especially useful for cutting the elaborate trim found on porches and balconies. The saw pictured in Fig. 2–10 is a Dremel Moto-Shop; it can be obtained with or without the accessories shown. The accessories include the sanding attachment, and a flexible shaft with an assortment of carving and grinding bits. It is very useful in making miniature furniture also. There are two sizes of sawblades available for this unit. The thinner blade is for very fine work, and the wider blade is recommended for scroll work. Either blade will produce a smooth cut and can be especially useful for cutting the square corners of doors and windows, if the table top is large enough to handle the size of the piece.

Dremel Moto-Tool

The Dremel Moto-Tool is extremely useful for shaping and carving ornate designs in wood. With the router bits and the available attachments, it can be used to produce the small cove and bead moldings that are often used as trim on miniature houses. It is available at most hobby and craft stores and a limited number of hardware stores.

Woodburning Pen

This desirable piece of equipment is used to add detail to various dollhouse components, such as the brick detail of a fireplace, or the ornate feature of the eave and roof brackets. It is also very useful in miniature furniture-making for producing a hand-carved appearance. The woodburning pen is available at hobby and craft stores, and can be equipped with several styles of pen tips to produce a variety of patterns. *Safe use of power tools cannot be over-emphasized.* The table saw pictures show the safety guard removed for clarity. This is not a recommended procedure for actual use. Accidents can and do happen, so use the safety devices that are provided by the manufacturer. Safety goggles are also important. Wear them and protect your eyes.

Hand Tools

Figures 2–12 and 2–13 show a selection of hand tools which are helpful for miniature work. The clamps are usually a necessity when working

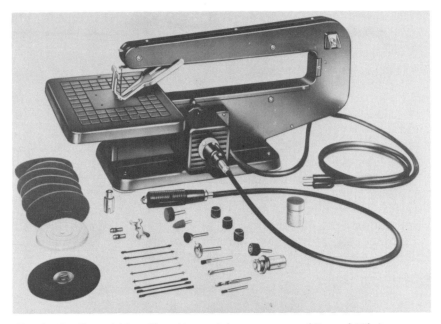

Fig. 2–10   Dremel Moto-Shop jigsaw (photo courtesy of Dremel Mfg.)

Fig. 2–11   Dremel Moto-Tool (photo courtesy of Dremel Mfg.)

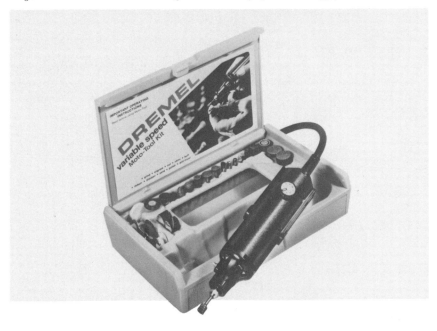

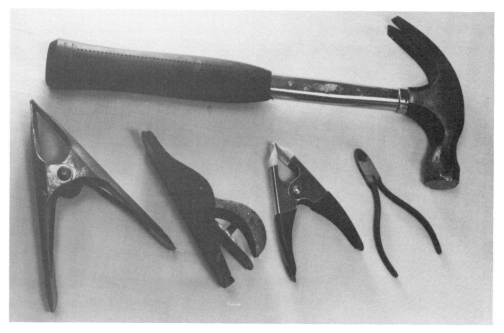

Fig. 2–12 *Hammer, spring clamps, plane, and wire cutters.*

Fig. 2–13 *Razor saw, X-Acto knives, pliers, and pin vise with small drill bit*

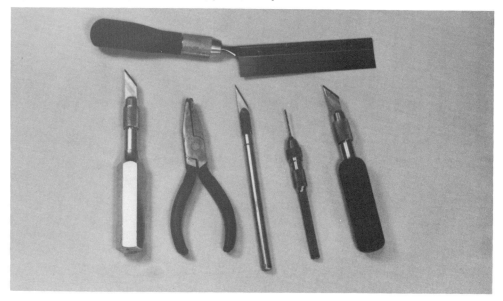

with tiny trim pieces. The craft knives are very helpful for cutting shingles to the desired shape to obtain a proper fit. The razor saw is extremely useful for cutting the trim molding for both the exterior and interior of the dollhouse. The pin vises, equipped with small drill bits, are used to predrill screw holes.

Many other small tools may be necessary at some phase of construction. Obtain these tools as the need arises. Specific hand tools are generally selected on the basis of availability and personal preference of the builder. The following hand tools are highly desirable, and are available at leading hardware stores, lumber yards, woodworking shops and a limited number of hobby and craft stores.

Hammer
Combination square or tri-square
Framing square
Ruler, 6 or 12-inch
Yardstick
Tape rule, 8 foot or longer
Glue clamps
C-clamps
Spring clamps
Hand saw or keyhole saw
Miter box
Back saw or razor saw
Knives (X-Acto #1 and #5)
Knife blades (X-Acto #11 and #24)
Flat and half-round files
Awl or ice pick
Screwdriver
Block plane
Dividers
Protractor
Scissors
Stapler
Tweezers
Router bits: cove cutters in $3/16$, $1/8$ and $3/32$-inch diameter bead cutters in $3/16$, $1/8$ and $3/32$-inch diameter
Drill bits: $3/8$ inch, $1/16$ inch and $1/8$-inch diameter
Dado blade

Framing Square

This is also called a carpenters square, and becomes very useful for pattern layout and squaring large pieces of plywood.

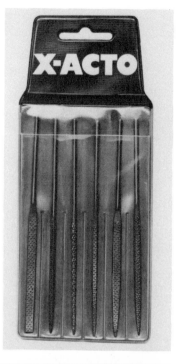

Fig. 2–14
Flat and half-round files (photo courtesy of X-Acto)

Fig. 2–15
Framing square, tri-square, ruler, and tape rule.

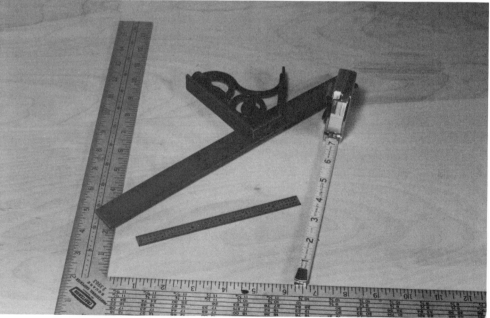

Tape Rule and Yardstick

These are essential tools, and accurate measurement is crucial when working with small pieces. Obtain high quality measuring devices.

Clamps

Wood clamps or C-clamps are especially useful when gluing and nailing together the walls, floors and the roof sections of the miniature house. They help by maintaining a tight fit and the proper alignment between parts until the glue has dried.

Spring clamps are helpful when installing house trim, shingles, siding, paneling, and rafter supports in maintaining alignment and proper fit. Because of the spring design, they are quick and easy to use.

Miter Box and Razor Saw

The small miter box and razor saw produced by X-Acto are shown in Fig. 2–16; they are ideal for cutting the thin pieces of architectural trim, including the chair rail, stair rail, picture frames, door and window casings. For the best results use the fine-tooth saw blade.

Awl or Ice Pick

Use these for scoring sheets of plastic, Lexan or Plexiglas, for the fabrication of miniature windows. The plastic panel can be scored and then bent along the score line to produce the desired size rather than cutting with a saw. The tools are also very useful for locating the position of holes to be drilled.

Block Plane

The block plane facilitates the edge trimming of plywood to produce a tight fit and flush joints at the corners of walls and roof sections.

Drill Bits

The 3/8-inch diameter drill bit is used for making starter holes for the sabre saw. Smaller sized bits can be used for making doweled joints, and for predrilling of screw holes.

Dado Blade

The dado blade is available in several different styles. It is primarily used for making a dado cut in the walls to support the floor sections, if desired. This act not only produces a tight fit, and increased strength, but also eliminates any gap between the walls and the floor sections.

Fig. 2–16   Miter box and razor saw (photo courtesy of X-Acto)

Stapler

A hand-held stapler is used for installing trim and siding on the house. Longer staples can be used in place of nails for the basic house construction also.

Additional Supplies

In addition to the power and hand tools, the following accessories will be extremely useful in miniature building.

Glue
Sandpaper, medium and fine grit
Pencils
Graph paper, ¼-inch grid
Carbon paper

BUILDINGS IN MINIATURE

Wood putty
Plastic foam paint brushes
Artists' brushes
Paint
Stain
Masking tape
Dowels, assorted sizes
Nails and brads, ¾-inch or 1-inch long
Butt hinges, ¾-inch size
Screws
Plastic for windows (Lexan or Plexiglas)

3
SCALE AND DIMENSIONS

Scale can be defined as the ratio of the reduced miniature dimension to the original full-sized measurement. There are several different scales used in miniature construction, but the scale most universally accepted as standard in the miniature world is the ¹⁄₁₂ scale. In this scale, 12 inches of actual measurement equal 1 inch of miniature measurement. This scale became accepted during the construction of the Dollhouse for Queen Mary of England in the early 1920's. *All* the craftspeople (some 450 men and women) had to work to the same scale to assure proper proportion between the various pieces.

At the completion of this tremendous project, the craftspeople continued to build miniatures to the accustomed scale. As the knowledge of their ability and the popularity of the Queen's Dollhouse spread throughout the world, so did the interest in miniatures, and the acceptance of the ¹⁄₁₂ scale as the standard scale. Recently there has been some interest shown in other size scales, predominantly the ½-inch scale. Limited amounts of miniature furniture have appeared in several areas in the eastern part of the country in both the ½-inch and the ¾-inch scale. However, the vast majority of the miniature houses, furniture and accessories that are being constructed today are built to the 1″ (¹⁄₁₂) scale.

In the United States, the basic unit of measurement for length is the inch. Parts of an inch can be expressed in two ways—fractional or decimal. All fractions have a decimal equivalent; for example, ¼ equals 0.25. Some craftspeople work with either method of expression, and some will prefer one system over the other. You should work in whatever system you are most accustomed to. The dimensions in the detailed plans and individual parts in this book are given in fractional form.

Converting Dimensions to Scale

When converting from the actual dimension to the scale dimension, first convert the foot, or feet, to the inch dimension and then any fraction of a foot to the corresponding fraction of an inch. For example, 4 feet 3 inches (or 4¼ feet) equals 4¼ inches.

The degree of accuracy required in establishing dimensions is largely a matter of choice. You can be as precise as you like, but precision to the nth degree is likely to be more trouble than it's worth. Using decimals will give you dimensions that are slightly more exact than fractions. Of course, you must then use a ruler that is marked in tenths or hundredths of an inch. You can also use an architect's rule, which does accurate conversions for you.

If you intend to build an exact replica of a specific house, such as your grandmother's house, or the one you currently are living in, or a specific one from the Historical Register, you must decide how precise your dimensions are to be. For example, suppose a room measures exactly 15 feet 10 inches; by rounding this dimension up to 16 feet, a very close approximation is obtained and working with the scale dimensions is greatly simplified. The amount of error that is produced by this rounding up will be approximately ⁵⁄₃₂ inch. To be practical when working with the scale dimensions, you may want to consider a slight compromise and round off the dimensions.

If you are making a replica of an older home, one that was built around the turn of the century, be aware that many of the components that went into the construction of this house, such as the windows and doors, were probably custom-made and may not necessarily fit any standard set of dimensions. Thus, obtaining standard miniature components to the exact dimensions of the house, in the full range of sizes required, may become a difficult task.

There are some features that cannot easily be reduced to the exact miniature scale without looking awkward or out of proportion. For instance, the first and second story floor thickness, on most older homes, is generally in excess of twelve inches thick. In the miniature house this looks completely out of scale.

Another feature that presents some problems when put in the miniature house is the floor to ceiling height. In the modern day home, the trend is to make the rooms with a lower ceiling height of 8 feet to conserve energy. However, when this lower height is reproduced in miniature, it produces a room with a cramped and dark atmosphere. It is better to utilize a 9- or 10-foot ceiling height to allow light to reach the far corners of the rooms.

Manufacturers have standardized the dimensions of most building components, like doors and windows. Most available miniature doors are 3 inches wide, which translates to a 3-foot width in actual dimension. Exterior entrance doors are indeed 3 feet wide, but most interior doors, such as bedroom, dining room and basement stairwell doors, are narrower, generally 30 inches wide. Closet doors range from 18 to 28 inches wide. If the width of an operating door has to be exact, you may want to consider fabricating your own. The existing door assemblies can be modified to obtain the desired dimensions also, by altering the casing material around the door in addition to changing the size of the door.

Obtaining Dimensions

There are several ways to determine close approximations of desired dimensions, when the features cannot actually be measured. It would be ideal if you could simply measure the actual house, but frequently details on the upper floors are inaccessible. And sometimes you must work completely from photographs. In these cases, you must use some method of estimation.

Projection Method

To obtain the height of a structure or the position of a certain feature on that structure, you can use the device shown in Fig. 3–1. To use the device, start by marking your exact eye level height on the building with a piece of masking tape or other easily seen marking. (The location of this marking will obviously depend on the height of the person doing the measuring.) For the purpose of this explanation, assume this height to be 5 feet above ground level. This mark will become the base point. Let's assume you want to determine the height of the roof ridge above the ground level. To establish this height, determine the exact spot where you must stand so that the line of sight along the bottom edge of the device is on the base point (eye level) of the building, and the line of sight over the top portion of the device is on the roof ridge. Next measure the distance between you and the base of the building. In this illustration the distance is 20 feet. To this distance of 20 feet add the height of the base point above ground, or 5 feet. This total of 25 feet is the height of the roof ridge above the ground level.

In this illustration, the height of the chimney can be measured from this same spot, but the chimney is taller than the roof ridge. Again measure the distance to the *base* of the chimney, which is 24 feet in this case and not 20 feet. Then add the height of the base point above ground level or 5 feet, and establish the height of the chimney to be 29 feet.

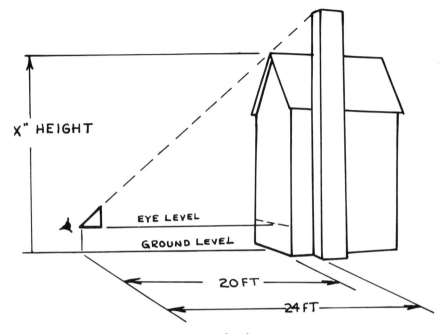

X" HEIGHT

EYE LEVEL

GROUND LEVEL

20 FT

24 FT

Fig. 3–1   Using projection to estimate height

By moving forward or backward, the height of any feature can be determined by the same process. Then *measure* the distance to the structure. This measured distance, plus the height to the base point or eye level indicator, will be the location height of the feature. The distance must always be measured from the point of sighting to a point directly under the feature. If the feature is located 6 feet *beyond* the front of the structure, you must add that 6 feet to the measured distance between you and the building.

To make the projection device, start with a piece of lumber or plywood and cut to the configuration shown in Fig. 3–2. Be sure that the base corner is square (90 degrees), and that both legs of the triangle are cut to the exact same length, in this case 12 inches. The longer the leg dimension is, the more accurate the projection measurement will be.

This system utilizes a 45 degree angle on each outside corner of the triangle in conjunction with a 90 degree base angle. When these conditions exist, the length of the legs of the established right triangle will be equal. Thus, the distance from you to the base point will be equal to the distance from the basepoint to the desired point. Remember you must then add the height of the base point. The projection system will not be

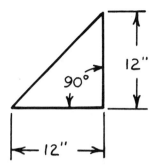

Fig. 3–2
Pattern for plywood projection device

accurate if the sighting is done on a slope or a hillside, because the angle between ground and structure will be in excess of 90 degrees. Always obtain the measurements from level ground.

Using Photographs

If it is impossible to physically measure the house, you can use photographs to approximate measurements. If you are taking the pictures yourself, place a yardstick right against the structure. It can then be used as the standard when figuring proportions. Always get the largest possible photo. You will be able to see more detail, and your dimensions will be more accurate.

Proportion Method

In order to use proportion to determine dimensions, you must know at least one measurement to use as a standard. In many houses, you can use a door or window, which you will assume to be 3 feet wide. If you have placed a yardstick in your photos, it can be used as the standard.

Using a graduated ruler, measure the width of the object you have designated to be the standard. The ratio of the photo standard to its actual measurement (expressed as $\frac{photo}{actual}$) will equal the ratio of any feature's photographic measurement to its actual measurement. For example, assume the yardstick is 1 inch long in the photo, and you want to determine the width of the building, which measures 8 inches in the photo. The ratio of the standard $\left(\frac{1\,(inch)}{3\,(feet)}\right)$ is equal to the width ratio $\left(\frac{8\,(inches)}{x\,(feet)}\right)$. Thus, $\frac{1}{3} = 8/x$. By crossmultiplying, you find that the house is 24 feet wide.

Another method that is almost as accurate is to measure the width of the house in the photograph and determine the number of times the standard will fit into that dimension. In the previous example it will fit exactly eight times. Knowing that the actual width of the standard is 3 feet, the house width can be established as 24 feet (3 feet × 8 equals 24 feet).

The same proportion method can be employed to establish dimensions for various items associated with the elevation or the height of the house, such as window height, eave location, height of the roof ridge, height of chimneys, balconies, and attic windows. In this case, use the measured *height* of a door (in the photograph) or some other *vertical* standard rather than the width of the standard. For close approximations, use a door height of 7 feet; for a more precise ratio use an 80-inch door height. The ratio is then set up the same as before to determine unknown heights. Avoid using horizontal features in a photograph to obtain vertical dimensions because of the distortion that can be caused by the angle of the camera. This distortion will only increase the amount of error.

Siding Proportions

Another method for obtaining a close approximation to any vertical dimension is to establish the height of *one* course of siding. The locations for various features on the house can then be determined by counting the number of courses of siding to the desired feature and then multiplying this number by the height of *one* course of siding. On most houses, the distance from the top of the foundation to the first story windowsill is approximately 3 feet. Count the number of courses from the foundation to the windowsill, and divide this number into 36 inches, thus getting the height of one course of siding can be established. This close approximation will be dependent upon the variations in the siding height.

Old houses often utilized a very narrow clapboard siding with a 3-inch overlap. Other old houses have an overlap of 4½ or 6 inches. On more modern houses the siding overlap can range from 8 to 12 inches. Recently built houses with the newer cedar shakes can have an overlap of as much as 14 inches. So if the number of siding courses between the foundation and the window sill is:

1. approximately three or slightly more, assume the overlap to be 12 inches for each course;
2. four or slightly more, assume the overlap to be 9 inches for each course;
3. six or slightly more, assume the overlap to be 6 inches per course;
4. eight or slightly more, assume that this is an older style siding with a 4½-inch overlap;
5. twelve or slightly more, assume this siding to be the very old style with a 3-inch overlap.

To verify this dimension, compare the number of courses of siding that are required to cover the height of the door. If the number of courses of siding required to cover the height of the door is:

1. seven, the overlap is approximately 12 inches;
2. nine, the overlap is approximately 9 inches;
3. thirteen to fourteen, the overlap is 6 inches;
4. nineteen to twenty-one, the overlap is 4½ inches.

Once the height of an individual course of siding has been established, the approximate height of other components can also be determined, such as the height of individual windows, the location of the eaves, or the height of the roof ridge.

Header Locations

Another dimension that can be used as a standard is the height of the door and window headers. It is the distance from the floor to the top of the window or door. This location is generally quite consistent regardless of the height of the window, or floor to ceiling dimension. Even shorter windows, associated with bathroom and kitchens, still have the top of the window, or header, located at the same height as a large window.

One of the few exceptions to this guideline is where there is a mixture of architectural styles, like a round-top Palladian window associated with a shorter Victorian or Federal window. In this case the top of the Palladian window will be above the normal header location of the adjacent window, and in this extreme case should not be used as a reference point. The height of the headers can be established with respect to a door header since the most usual height for a door is 6 feet 8 inches (rounded up to 7 feet, for simplicity). With this known dimension, other feature locations can be determined.

Avoid if possible the windowsill location for windows located in the living room. They generally have a variety of dimensions due to picture windows, bay windows and standard-sized windows all being in the same room. The windows flanking a fireplace or built-in bookshelves vary in the location of the window sill also. Stained glass windows were generally not built to consistent dimensions either.

If the house has a series of steps either at the front entrance or at the service door, then these can sometimes be used to establish other dimensions. Generally steps are installed to the standard dimension of 8 inches for each step riser. This dimension should be used only if there is a series of steps, and should not be used if there is only one or two steps. A single step was installed to accomodate the porch floor height, or the height of the stoop, and could be any size.

4
CONSTRUCTION TECHNIQUES AND TERMS

Every craftsperson has his or her favorite method of doing something. As this method becomes refined through application, the craftsperson gains a degree of expertise, in this particular method. This in turn is classified as an individual's technique. Different people develop various techniques or methods of doing an operation. They know what works well for them because of their experience. The techniques explained in this chapter are merely methods of doing a particular activity. There are many other equally valid methods of accomplishing the same operation. Utilize any approach you feel more comfortable with; there are no right or wrong methods of doing things in the miniature world.

Design

Room Arrangement
If a specific room arrangement is not a rigid requirement, consider arranging the individual rooms to fit the full depth of the miniature house. This arrangement will simplify the construction and makes the house much easier to decorate with paint or wallpaper.

Small Rooms
Small rooms—bathrooms, dressing rooms, dens and closets—can be increased in size slightly by substituting a thinner material for the interior wall sections. If a ⅜-inch plywood is used for the basic house construction, by replacing the interior partitions with a ¼ or ⅛-inch panel the

length and the width of the small room will be increased without affecting the remaining dimensions of the other rooms in the house.

Removable Partitions

Interior wall sections or partitions that are removable will allow for variations in the furniture arrangement as well as variations in room arrangement. Removable partitions also facilitate interior decorating, which is a great benefit to the miniature builder. They also allow for a more flexible floor plan by permitting the room sizes and shapes to vary.

Floor-to-Ceiling Height

Increasing the normal 8-inch floor-to-ceiling dimension to 9 or 10 inches permits more light to enter the far corners of the rooms. This is especially needed for long rooms, where the back may be in complete darkness. Consider including a bay window or a library window for additional light.

Flat Roof

Consider utilizing a flat-roof on your house, like a San Francisco Victorian, if cutting the complicated roof angles are a problem. It not only eliminates the required angle cutting for the roof sections, but also the tedious task of shingling the roof. The top story will have more space than an attic section located at the same level.

Porches

When establishing the size of the porch floor, allow for a sufficient area to permit the addition of a porch swing or other outdoor furniture at a later date. Once the house has been built, it is very difficult to increase the size of the porch without altering some other feature on the miniature house.

Recess the porch foundation wall at least ⅜ inch from the outer floor edge to allow for the addition of lattice trim later. If this recess is not left at the beginning of the construction stage, the lattice will protrude from the foundation and have an adverse effect on the appearance of the miniature house.

Dust Cover

In addition to backing all windows with plastic, consider using a large sheet as a dust cover for the open side of the miniature house. It can be backed with a thin layer of a soft plastic or cork at the edges of the house, to make it almost air tight. When you consider the difficulty in dusting all those tiny details and the time involved, it becomes quite apparent that the dust cover would be highly desirable.

Construction

Layout

When doing the layout on a sheet of plywood, use a carpenters' framing square or a dry wall square to assure squareness of the pattern with the edge of the plywood panel. Measuring and marking the same dimension on each edge of the panel and then connecting those lines will not guarantee that the pattern is square.

Cutting

When cutting duplicate pieces on thin stock, like porch brackets, tape several pieces of wood together with masking tape and cut with a jigsaw for more consistency of pattern between parts.

If at all possible, cut all pieces that have the same width or length at one time to assure maximum uniformity. This is especially helpful for partitions on the same story of the house. It eliminates any error in resetting the dimension on the rip fence of the table saw.

Gluing

Always remove excess glue as soon as possible, while the glue is still wet. This is especially important on the inside partitions where access is very limited, to assure a smooth surface for installing wallpaper, paneling or wainscoting, and painting.

Installing Floor Tile

In order to obtain a smooth, flat surface when installing floor tile in the room of a miniature house, place tile in proper position and apply a weight to the top surface until the glue has dried. This will prevent any shifting or curling of the tile and produce a uniform pattern to the tile.

Doors and Windows

Opening Cutouts

To assure that a window or door opening is located squarely with the wall panel, first cut out only the outline of the wall section and dry assemble this section to the house to assure squareness and proper fit. Once the proper fit of the wall section has been established, then locate the door or window openings with a framing square (Fig. 4–1).

Once the location and the outline of the openings have been finalized, the cutout can be made with a sabre saw. First use an electric drill with a ⅜-inch wood bit to drill four holes, one in each corner of the required opening (Fig. 4–2). These holes are starting holes for the sabre saw blade.

For exterior windows *only*, the cutouts can be done after the house has been assembled, providing that sufficient access space is available for the sabre saw. All interior doors, arches and exterior doors must be cut out before assembling the structure. For ease of assembly, make the openings ⅟16 inch larger than the component size, for both the length and the width.

Window Layout

A large number of windows may have tremendous eye appeal on the exterior of the house, but it makes furniture arrangement much more difficult, and seriously curtails the number of pictures and wall hangings you have space for.

Locate windows away from the corners, so that the corner area can be used for structural support, unless it is a bay window or library window that is required to be located at the corner. A window at the extreme corner of a house will also present problems for applying trim and siding.

Door Layout

The final location of a door requires careful consideration or problems can ensue. When a door is opened, it should not block another door opening, window, hallway opening or stairway. Allow sufficient space for the door to function properly, whether it is a right-handed or left-handed door. Placing the location too close to a corner may prevent the installation of the door casing, on both the interior and exterior. A corner location can also affect the installation of siding on the exterior of the house as well as the corner caps.

In a house that requires an extensive number of exterior or interior doors, some builders prefer to substitute a false-front door in leiu of an exterior operating door to conserve the amount of interior wall space. A false-front door is assembled on only one side of a wall, while the other side of the wall is blank. It gives the impression of a door where none exists. The false-front door permits more floor space for a variety of furniture arrangements, and more wall space for pictures, mirrors and other wall hangings.

It can be produced to any desired size, but the most preferred size is the standard miniature door, with dimensions of 3 inches wide and 7 inches high (Fig. 4–3). The individual door components can be purchased, including the raised panels; or you can make the individual pieces

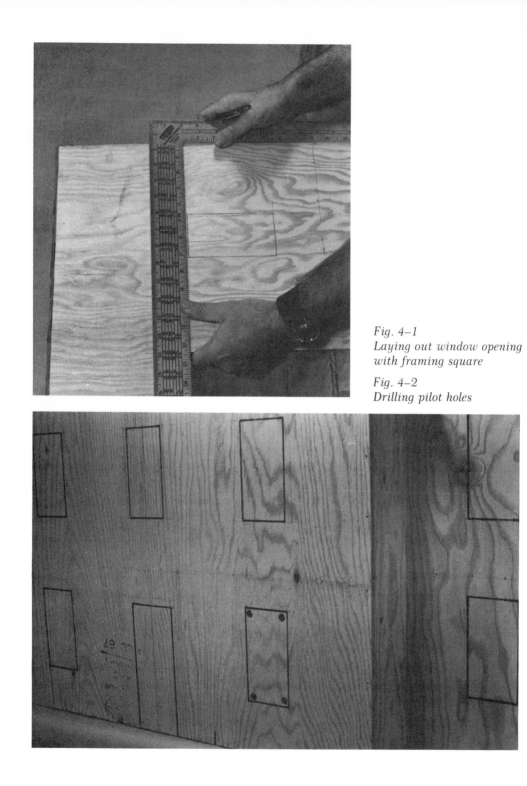

Fig. 4–1
*Laying out window opening
with framing square*

Fig. 4–2
Drilling pilot holes

Fig. 4–3
False-front door

from scratch. Attach the required pieces in position with glue. Stain door to the desired color and attach a door knob on the exterior side only.

Walls

Angled Walls

If your house design calls for angled walls, such as the living room and sun porch later in this book, or if you are building your own bay windows, you must be able to calculate the outside length of the beveled pieces.

Fig. 4–4 shows two walls which meet at a 135 degree angle (or 45 degrees from the horizontal). You need to find the length of "X", which can be done trigonometrically. The tangent of angle 22½° is equal to side "X" divided by the width ⅜ inch (or .375 inch). By using a calculator or consulting a tangent table, you can find that the tangent of 22½° is 0.4142. Substituting it into the equation gives you $.4142 = \frac{X}{.375}$, so X equals .1553 or 5/32 inch.

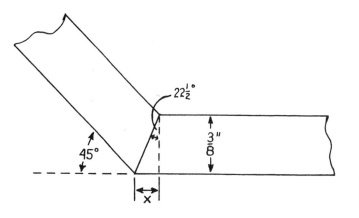

Fig. 4–4
Bevel cuts for angled walls

Therefore you know that each bevel cut will add 5/32 inch to the overall length of the piece. This method can be used for any wall angle. Several other commonly used tangents are:

15°   0.2679
20°   0.3640
30°   0.5774
45°   1.0000

Hinged Wall

Placing the hinges on a wall section can be a major concern. With few exceptions any front corner is suitable for mounting a hinge. Care must be taken with the wall area under the roof overhang, so that the pivoting section will clear the eave. Allow for a full 90-degree pivot of the section so that it does not interfer with another portion of the miniature house when being opened.

Any protruding section of the house can be a potential obstruction to the pivot wall; check clearance carefully. A bay window, porch, balcony, chimney or eave brackets are all conspicuous areas of concern. The wall should have good firm support on both sides of the movable section. If the hinged section is extremely large or heavy, consideration should be given to supporting the wall in both the closed and the open position to reduce the strain on the hinges.

The horizontal gap at the top of a hinged section can be made inconspicuous by adding some architectural trim. The vertical gaps can be minimized by installing a magnetic cabinet latch to assure a tight fit. Mount the hinges on the corners and allow the corner trim boards and siding to help conceal the gap between the walls and also to conceal the hinges.

Exterior Wall Bevels

Where the outside walls of the miniature house join the roof section, a sturdier and more appealing structure can be obtained by beveling the edge of the exterior wall to match the existing roof angle. This will improve the strength of the house by creating a larger bonding area for the roof panel. An example of the exterior wall section that has been beveled to match the roof angle is shown in Fig. 4–5.

Wallpapering

Prior to installing wallpaper, seal the wood with a light coat of paint or shellac to smooth out the irregularities on the surface for better adhesion of the paper. When paint is dry sand lightly with a fine grade of sandpaper. Use rubber cement or the wallpaper paste designed specifically for miniature work to attach the paper to the wall. Apply quickly and spread evenly to avoid bubbles in the wallpaper. Do not try to cover too large an area at one time. Limit your work to one wall at a time, so pattern can be matched with adjoining wall.

Fig. 4–5   Bevel on exterior wall

A regular white wood glue can be used also; mix glue with an equal amount of water and apply with a brush or sponge. Then attach the wallpaper, removing bubbles as you go.

For inexpensive wallpaper contact interior decorating shops or paint stores and obtain the discarded wallpaper pattern books. Not all the patterns are useful, but many of the small patterns can be used for bathrooms, closets or small accent areas, lining drawers and chests, or for borders with existing paper. Some of the cloth patterns can be used to simulate upholstered furniture.

Wainscot Molding

Wainscot molding trim is generally used to cap the top of wainscot paneling used on the lower wall section and to provide a chair rail stop. It can be used as a chair rail without the wainscoting, and can also be used as a substitute for picture frame molding, especially the ornate cap variety.

Roof

Installing Shingles

When installing shingles use a yardstick or a similar strip of wood for aligning a complete row of shingles at one time. This will greatly reduce the amount of time required to apply the shingles and assure a neat straight row. Using spring clamps at each end of the yardstock will also expedite the task of shingling, by permitting both hands to be free.

Hinged Roof

Roof sections are generally hinged to permit access to the attic, which is often used for storage. The best location for the hinges on the roof section is about two to three inches below the ridge. This permits additional strength at the ridge, created by gluing the two roof sections together. If the house contains a chimney or a cupola, allow sufficient roof space between it and the hinges.

Roof Supports

To improve the structural strength of any miniature house or building, add additional supports to the roof as shown in Figs. 4–6 and 4–7. This not only strengthens the roof section but also creates a larger bonding surface. The supports can be fabricated from any scrap pieces of plywood or lumber available. Fit the supports flush with the roof angle of the wall and attach with glue and nails. Apply glue clamps or spring clamps until the glue has dried.

Fig. 4–6   Roof supports

Fig. 4–7   Roof supports

Fascia Boards and Roof Trim

Adding fascia boards and roof trim boards to the edges of the roof sections will greatly improve the appearance of the miniature house by concealing the exposed plywood edges of the roof sections. The addition of these boards adds a finished look.

Eave Brackets

Due to the limited number of commercial eave brackets available, you may be compelled to fabricate your own, if a specific style of eave bracket is required. It can be a very easy and simple task if you possess a router. You can also use the accessory end of a radial saw, with either a ¼-inch or a ⅜-inch bead cutting router bit.

On a ⅜-inch thick by 1 inch wide board, cut the edge with the selected router bit to produce the bead shaped molding. Then utilize a table or radial saw and cut strip of lumber crosswise into ½-inch pieces until the desired number of brackets are obtained. Glue two pieces together to form the letter L as shown in Fig. 4–8. To increase the length of the bracket, adjust the width of the board prior to the routing operation and then adjust the saw cut width to obtain brackets of various widths.

To add a slightly novel effect, utilize a ¼-inch drill and drill a hole about ³/₃₂ inch deep at the top on both sides of the bracket. The side surface of the brackets can also be finished by either chip carving, painting or adding a unique rosette feature. An exceptionally pleasing effect can be obtained by using upholsterers' tacks as rosettes. These can be painted to match or painted a contrasting color to accent the eave bracket design. Another variation of style can be obtained by combining a bead style molding with a cove shaped molding to obtain the bracket shown in Fig. 4–9.

Smaller sized cove and bead molding cutters can be used to produce some small and delicate eave brackets. These cutter bits can be obtained

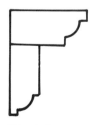

Fig. 4–8
Eave bracket

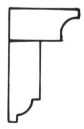

Fig. 4–9
Eave bracket

Fig. 4–10
Ornate eave brackets

at most hobby and craft stores, and are available in ³⁄₁₆, ⅛ and ³⁄₃₂-inch diameters.

Other eave brackets can be made from ¼-inch material. A jigsaw can be utilized to cut out the desired pattern (Fig. 4–10). To obtain eave brackets of an exceptionally wide width, first cut several individual brackets with a jigsaw from ⅛-inch stock and then glue several pieces together to obtain the desired width.

Attic

When the attic roof is exposed to view, scaled rafters can be added at 2-inch intervals to resemble an unfinished attic roof. These rafters should be ⁵⁄₃₂ inch thick and ½ inch wide, and extend the length of the roof, from the roof ridge to the eave.

Room dividers utilized in the attic can be used for roof support if cut to the roof shape. This will eliminate the long unsupported span of the roof, and will increase the structural integrity of the miniature house.

Staircases

If a purchased staircase does not exactly fit the floor-to-ceiling height in the house, due to a thick floor section or an odd dimension, place a landing at the base of the stairwell if the height variation is less than a full step riser height. The variation can be compensated for in the height of the landing, to eliminate the tedious task of completely rebuilding the staircase. This was the method employed during the construction of many older houses (built around the turn of the century) to accommodate for the variations in the floor-to-ceiling height between the different rooms.

Head Height Clearance

When considering the layout for a staircase, allow for the proper head height clearance (7 feet actual or 7 inches in scale) at any landing or at the top of the stairs, to maintain the proper proportion. This height should be maintained over a 3-inch (scale) minimum square area in both places, the top of the stairs and on any landing of the staircase. Also consider the head height clearance when locating a staircase under a roof section of the miniature house. This height should be a minimum of 6½ inches in scale to maintain a realistic resemblence to the actual height in a full sized house. In a small dollhouse or in cramped quarters it is difficult to maintain this clearance unless the steps are made very steep. If this is the situation, consider eliminating the staircase altogether, rather than installing a noticeably extra-steep staircase. Where space is limited, consider using a staircase with a landing and change direction 180 degrees if necessary. An open-style staircase should be used if at all possible, because it permits more light into the room.

Custom Staircases

Staircase construction in a miniature house can be accomplished in the same manner as for a full-sized house. The only difference is the dimensions that are used; the method is identical.

In the construction of a staircase for a regular sized house, there is a standard practice for generating the shape of the staircase stringers. (The stringers are the supporting elements of the individual stair riser and tread.) The shape of the staircase stringer is the result of establishing the stair riser *height* and the stair tread *depth*.

The rule-of-thumb method consists of utilizing 17½ inches as the basic industry standard. This dimension is the combined measurement of one stair riser height plus the dimension of one stair tread depth, as the standard dimension. There are two combinations of dimensions that predominate in the industry. One combination is a stair riser of 8½ inches used with a stair tread of 9 inches. The other common combination is a stair riser with an 8-inch height and a stair tread with a 9½-inch depth.

The staircase in this example must fit a floor-to-ceiling height of 9½ inches. To this you must add the second-story floor thickness of ⅜ inch, for a total height of 9⅞ inches. At this point the *actual* dimensions will be converted to the 1/12 scale dimension in the *decimal* form for ease of calculation.

Each *inch* in actual dimension is equal to 1/12 or .083 inch in scale dimension. Therefore a step riser (actual) of 8½ inches equals .7055 inch in scale, and a step tread (actual) of 9 inches equals .747 inch in scale, so the combined total (actual) of 17½ inches = 1.4525 inches in scale.

To determine the number of steps required for the staircase, divide the staircase height (9.875 inches) by the step riser height (.7055 inch) to give a result of 13.997, rounded up to 14.

For the most accuracy do the actual layout with full-scale dimensions. Start the actual staircase layout as shown in Fig. 4–11, with two parallel lines, A and B, spaced 9.875 inches apart. Then with one end of a yardstick or 18-inch ruler placed on the bottom line and the 14-inch mark on the top line, draw horizontal lines at each inch increment as indicated. Next, draw fourteen perpendicular lines between the two parallel lines at ³⁄₄-inch spacings (to represent the stair tread width of 9 inches) starting at the position of the 14-inch mark on line A (Fig. 4–12). Then connect the horizontal lines with the appropriate vertical lines and the pattern for the staircase stringer is complete (Fig. 4–13).

This method of generating the shape of the staircase stringer can be used for any floor-to-ceiling height, by adjusting the overall height of the staircase to compensate for the change in the floor to ceiling height dimension. If the layout drawing is done in full scale, at the completion of the layout the pattern for the stringer is ready to be transferred to a piece of lumber and cut out.

Transfer the pattern to a ¼ inch thick (or more) by 1 inch wide piece of lumber with carbon paper. Then cut out two identical stringer patterns with a jigsaw. The stair risers and stair treads can be fabricated from standard ³⁄₃₂-inch stock material, cut to the desired length. The dimension of the stair riser height will be the .7055-inch dimension that was established earlier. The stair tread width will have to be increased, from the previously established .75 inch to allow for the thickness of the stair riser, and also to produce an overlap as shown in Fig. 4–14. This increase in dimension can be approximately ³⁄₃₂ to ⅛ inch, depending on the amount of overlap desired. The length of the individual stair risers and stair treads will be determined by the desired overall *width* of the staircase.

If an open staircase is desired, obtain the necessary balusters, newel posts and railings. Cut the individual pieces to the desired dimensions; stain to the desired color, and install with glue. Remove the excess glue immediately. When glue has dried apply a final finish coat with small brush or a spray can. Use a satin finish to obtain a semi-gloss sheen. Apply a second coat of finish if desired, after the first coat has dried.

Painting or Staining

The task of painting or staining dollhouse components such as doors, windows, staircases, wainscoting, chair rail molding, flooring, and other moldings is greatly simplified by working on the individual pieces prior to assembling them. Painting the windows before attaching to the house eliminates the possibility of paint smears on the siding. Staining the wainscoting or panel trim and allowing it to completely dry before in-

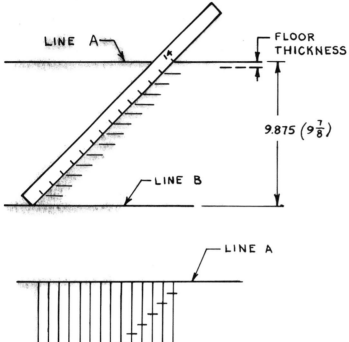

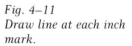

Fig. 4–11
Draw line at each inch
mark.

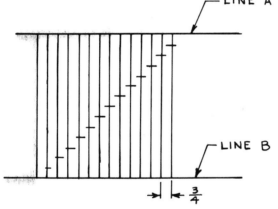

Fig. 4–12
Draw fourteen vertical lines.

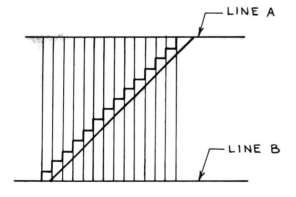

Fig. 4–13
Completed stringer pattern

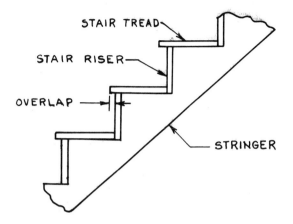

Fig. 4–14
Staircase construction

stalling prevents the stain from marking the adjoining wallpaper or paint. Because staircases are generally located toward the middle of the house, it is much more convenient to remove the staircase from the house during the staining and finishing.

When painting or staining very thin sections of wood like siding, wainscoting, or flooring, apply a weight or glue clamp to the wood to prevent warping until dry. Warping will occur when gluing these sections in place also, so again use a weight or clamps until the glue has dried.

To facilitate the painting of doors and windows with permanently installed glass panes, mask off the glass area on both sides of the window sash with masking tape. Utilize a vinyl or acrylic paint for easy clean up with water and soap. Avoid using a razor blade to remove paint smears on plastic window pane because it tends to scratch very easily.

Terminology

The terms used in this book are generally for an explicit item or construction detail. A cross-sectional view of a house showing various structural details can be observed in Fig. 4–15. This view will help in the comprehension of terminology used here and in the other sections of this book.

Windows and Doors

JAMB—The upright or vertical member that supports a window or a door.
LIGHT—The number of lights indicates the total number of panes of glass in the window.

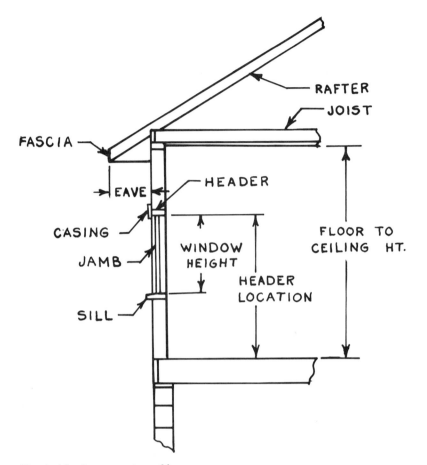

Fig. 4–15   Cross-section of house

SASH—The framework in a door or window that supports or contains the window panes.

SILL—The horizontal member at the base of the window or door.

HEADER—The horizontal member at the top of the window or door which supports the framework.

CASING—The molding used to enclose doors or windows both on the interior and exterior of the house.

TRANSOM—The small window or shutter panel located over a door or window.

DOUBLE-HUNG WINDOW—A window in which the bottom portion can move up and the top portion can move down in separate tracks.

FIXED-SASH WINDOW—A non-movable window, such as some bay windows, picture windows, or attic windows.

THRESHOLD—The horizontal member which forms the base of the door and supports the framework.

Roof

GABLE—The vertical, triangular shaped end of a building from the eaves to the roof ridge.

ROOF RIDGE—The intersection at the top of the roof, where the two roof planes meet.

GAMBREL—A style of roof referred to as a "barn roof," composed of two sections with the lower section having a slope steeper than the upper section.

MANSARD—A style of roof like a flat roofed A-frame where the lower section has a steeper slope than the upper section.

DORMER—The roofed structure for a window located in the roof section.

SHED—A type of roof with only one slope from front to back.

EAVE—The lower portion of a roof that overhangs the wall.

SOFFIT—The underside part of the roof overhang or eave.

PITCH—The degree or angle of the slope of the roof.

FASCIA—The front trim board located at the outside edge of the eave.

Staircase

STRINGER—The supporting member of the stairs, generally notched to hold the individual stair risers and treads.

STAIR RISER—The vertical height of one step in the staircase.

STAIR TREAD or RUN—The horizontal width of one step in the staircase.

NEWEL POST—The post located at the base of the staircase, or on the landing or at the top of the stairs as a support for the stair railing.

BANNISTER or BALUSTER—The upright supporting posts of the handrail.

Saw Cuts

KERF—A narrow groove in a piece of wood, generally the width of a single cut with the sawblade.

DADO—A wide cut in a board to match the thickness of a joining board to form a tight joint. This type of cut can be obtained with several passes with a single sawblade or with a single pass with the wide dado head cutter.

MITER—A cut obtained by cutting a board at an angle.

BEVEL—A bevel cut is obtained by cutting the edge of a board at a slant.

COMPOUND BEVEL or COMPOUND CUT—The combination of a miter cut and a bevel cut. It is obtained by cutting the board at an angle and at a slant simultaneously.

Fig. 4–16
Moldings

Miscellaneous Terms

EXTERIOR WALL—An outer support wall exposed to the elements, used to support the roof load.

PARTITION—Any inside wall, generally non-load-bearing.

SUPPORT WALL or LOAD-BEARING WALL—An interior partition that supports some of the roof weight and thereby distributes the load more evenly.

FLOOR PLAN—A detailed and dimensioned layout, showing wall arrangement, locations of doors, windows and other construction features of the house or building in the horizontal plane.

ELEVATION VIEWS—A layout of the exterior walls and interior partitions that show the locations and heights of doors, windows, fireplaces, stairwells and special built-in features in the vertical plane.

Architectural Trim

Architectural trim is available in many ready-made shapes in various types of wood, and also in plastic on some items. A majority of miniature builders utilize the wooden products and only resort to the plastic trim when a very intricate pattern is desired and is not available in the wooden form.

Some of the basic shapes of precut molding, which are readily available, are shown in a cross-sectional view in Fig. 4–16. The basic shapes include: (1) cove molding; (2) bead molding; (3) quarter-round and (4) half-round. Molding shapes are also available for clapboard siding, baseboards, door casings, chair rails and picture frame materials. The selection of picture frame molding is quite extensive, ranging in width from $\frac{1}{8}$ inch up to $\frac{3}{8}$ inch. It is available in various styled contours including some that are very ornate. A majority of the pre-cut moldings are produced from basswood or pine, which makes them easy to cut, stain and finish.

Symbols

Shown in Fig. 4–17 are a few basic symbols that are used in architecture. By utilizing these symbols in data collecting and in the process of developing the floor plans, you will maintain consistency between all levels of the development of the floor plans. To distinguish between the interior and the exterior doors, the threshold that is shown applies to the exterior doors only and is located on the exterior side of the structure. This is very

DOORS

INTERIOR, R.H.

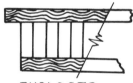

EXTERIOR, R.H.

STAIRCASE

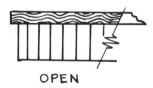

ENCLOSED

OPEN

WINDOWS

MOVABLE
SASH

FIXED
SASH

FIREPLACE

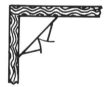

PLAN VIEW

BUILT IN

WALLS

WOOD

BRICK

ARCHWAY

BEVEL CUT

END

FRONT

BACK

Fig. 4–17   Architectural symbols

helpful in the orientation of the floor plan when attempting to construct the overall layout of each story in the house sometime after the original sketch was made. Also note the right-hand indication.

Another significant symbol is the one used to distinguish between the fixed sash windows and the operating or movable sash window. The windowsill extends beyond the wall to denote the house exterior.

For the staircases, the complete number of steps need not be indicated in the sketch. This quantity can be identified in the note specifying the stair riser height and the stair tread depth. The symbols for wood and brick walls can be indicated as shown or with a note.

The symbol for indicating the bevel cut will be utilized frequently in pattern layout. This symbol indicates to which side of the panel the bevel belongs, top or bottom. This is especially important if the panel is odd shaped, or if the plywood panel has only one good side. On square or rectangular pieces it is also important if the door or window openings have already been installed.

The symbol for the fireplace is primarily used to indicate the relative position in a room. Actual or scaled dimensions of the fireplace could be included on the floor plan or on a separate sketch of the fireplace to show more of the detail. If it is an ornate fireplace, additional sketches should be included, also.

The symbol for the built-in should be identified as a china cabinet or bookcase or whatever. Doors are depicted here. An elevation view or a note should be included to indicate the height of the cabinet doors, the number and spacing of the shelves and the overall height.

Abbreviations

Abbreviations are used to reduce the amount of writing required when obtaining notes and dimensions for the various details of the actual house construction. They are also exceptionally useful on drawings and detailed sketches where space is extremely limited. The following abbreviations are used in the detailed layouts, floor plans, elevation views and the individual part drawings.

Cl	Ceiling
Clo	Closet
₵	On center of part
D or Dia	Diameter
Dim	Dimension
Fl	Floor
Ht	Height

Loc	Location
Lt	Lights, window panes
R or Rad	Radius, Radii
Typ	Typical of several features
W	Width
Win	Window
Kit	Kitchen
D.R.	Dining Room
L.R.	Living Room
B.R.	Bedroom
M.B.R.	Master Bedroom
L	Length
R.H.	Right Hand
L.H.	Left Hand

5
BUILDING COMPONENTS

You can build your miniature house as small and compact as you desire or as large and elaborate as you can imagine—anything from a single-room display box to a 20-room, 4-story Victorian. The amount of minute detail that you incorporate into the construction of the basic house is a matter of personal preference.

Once you have established the basic shape and size of your house, you can produce any design or style merely by changing the architectural trim and adding details. By altering the roof line, adding a porch, removing or adding a bay window, or altering the style of the door and window trim, you can transform the house into a completely different architectural style.

This section will identify the various styles of architecture to help you select the one that suits your particular taste. The various miniature architectural components that are commercially available include the Victorian and the San Francisco Victorian, the Palladian, and the York-town styles. Plain style trim, called Early American or Colonial style, and which was typical of that era in the New England states, is also widely available.

Today there is almost an unlimited variety of building material available for the do-it-yourselfer, from doors and windows to scale bricks with actual mortar. You can buy everything from $\frac{1}{32}$-inch Lexan plastic for windows to a myriad of wood moldings which will satisfy the most discerning craftspeople. The assortment of ready-made moldings includes the quarter-round, half-round, chair rail, cove molding, door and window casing, jamb, siding, shingles, eave supports and gutters, just to mention a few (Fig. 5–1).

Wood turnings in a variety of shapes and sizes for construction of porches and balconies and staircases are also available. Figures 5–2 and 5–3 show various newel posts, balusters, spindles and bedposts, ranging in size from ⅜ inch to 12 inches. The veranda spindles shown in Fig. 5–4 are 2 inches long, and the porch spindles in Fig. 5–5 have ¼-inch diameter by 2⅝ inches long.

It may be helpful to obtain one or more catalogs from miniatures suppliers before establishing the final dimensions on your miniature house. In that way you will know the standard sizes of all components, including the doors and windows, that are available in your chosen style of architecture. With the dimensions of the individual components, allowances can be made to accomodate those dimensions into your plan at an early stage. A list of suppliers is included later in this chapter.

Doors

Both exterior and interior doors are available in a variety of styles, in kit or pre-assembled form. A Yorktown style door (also called Federal or Jamestown) is shown in Fig. 5–6. This is an operating door that opens to the right side; it is fabricated from basswood for easy staining or painting. The Yorktown requres an opening size of 3⅜ inches wide by 7⁷⁄₁₆ inches high.

The Victorian styled door shown in Fig. 5–7 requires an opening size of 3⅜ inches wide by 8⁵⁄₁₆ inches high. This door is an operating door that opens on the left side and swings to the right. It is primarily fabricated from basswood, which eases the staining and painting. This door also contains a Victorian styled transom above the door, and an ornate door cap above the transom. The six raised panels on the door proper add depth to this attractive design.

The elegant Palladian style shown in Fig. 5–8 requires an opening size of 3⁵⁄₁₆ inches wide by 8¹¹⁄₁₆ inches high (this will require a radius cut at the top and not a square cut as the rest of the doors do). The large semi-circular shaped transom above the door can be converted to a stain glass window by the addition of small fan-shaped pieces of colored glass or plastic, as can the glass panel in the door proper. This door is also fabricated from basswood for easy staining or painting. This door is hinged on the right side and is an operating door.

The ornate San Francisco Victorian style door shown in Fig. 5–9 requires an opening of 3⅜ inches wide by 10⁵⁄₁₆ inches high. It is an extremely tall door and requires a larger-than-normal floor to ceiling height. It also contains an elaborate amount of ornate trim, which is typical of the actual houses located on Nob Hill in San Francisco. It is

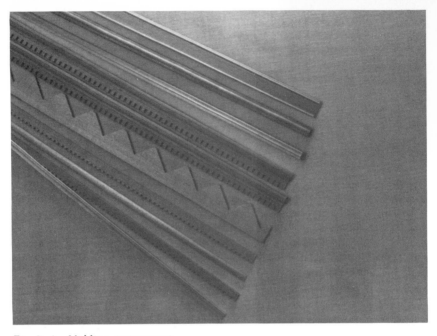

Fig. 5–1   Molding assortment

Fig. 5–2   Commercially available wood turnings

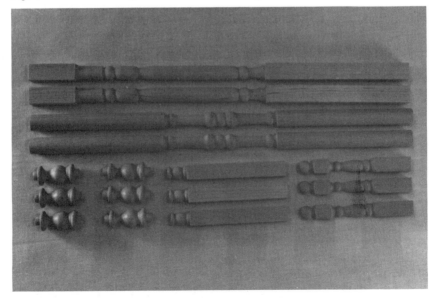

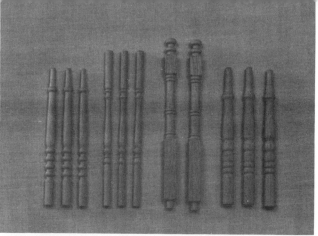

Fig. 5–3
Newel posts and balusters

Fig. 5–4
Veranda spindles

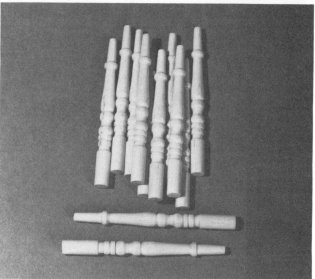

Fig. 5–5
Porch spindles (photo courtesy of Houseworks, Inc.)

Fig. 5–6
Yorktown style door (photo courtesy of Houseworks, Inc.)

Fig. 5–7
Victorian style door

Fig. 5–8
Palladian style door (photo courtesy of Houseworks, Inc.)

Fig. 5–9
San Francisco Victorian style door (photo courtesy of Houseworks, Inc.)

a style that is peculiar to the Bay Area. It is fabricated primarily from basswood and is a right-handed door. The long narrow glass pane and the raised panel in the lower door makes an attractive addition to any miniature house.

The Crossbuck Country style shown in Fig. 5–10 requires an opening size of 3¹⁄₁₆ inches wide by 7⁹⁄₁₆ inches high. This door is also fabricated from basswood for ease in painting or staining. The four-light transom can be used for plain glass or a stained glass unit, as can the main door section. This is also a right-handed door.

The Crossbuck Dutch door shown in Fig. 5–11 has two separate sections which operate independently of each other. This style door will add country charm to any style miniature house.

Additional styles of doors that are commercially available include the double French door and double doors for most of the above styles, plus several styles of interior doors. Some contain raised wood panels, others contain glass, while still others are the plain modern type, devoid of trim. Elaborate frames, for both doors and windows, which contain an overhead stained glass transom may require a minimum floor-to-ceiling height of

Fig. 5–10
Crossbuck country style door

Fig. 5–11
Crossbuck dutch style door

10 inches. When the ornate curved Palladian style is considered, the floor-to-ceiling height should be increased to approximately 12 inches. When establishing a higher floor-to-ceiling height, remember to consider the height of the staircase which will be required.

The most significant advantage to purchasing ready-made doors is the amount of time saved in the overall construction and assembly of the miniature house. This time saved can be extensive when you consider the number of doors found in a tall and expansive house. Utilizing ready-made doors also eliminates the need for many expensive tools used to produce the door panels and the ornate trim. It also eliminates the need for an extensive inventory, of both wood and glass, to produce the desired style door.

The most important disadvantage of ready-made doors is the size limitations. With a few exceptions, most of the doors produced today are 3 inches by 7 inches. This is very acceptable for exterior doors, but if you are a purist these dimensions will be oversized for most interior doors. They can be made smaller by modifying the door and frame, however. My only other objection is the fact that all the doors have right-hand opening. Here again, they can be altered with a little effort by changing the location of the top and bottom hinge pins from the right side of the door to the left side.

Windows

There are probably more variations in the styles and sizes of miniature windows than in any other building component. They range in size from the small attic window to the large side-by-side double units. Windows are available with operating sash or fixed sash, with or without "glass" (plastic) panes and in kit form or ready-made units. Also available are casement windows and slide-by units and windows with shutters attached. Or if you prefer, you can buy the trim, window jamb, sash, still, header and casing material and fabricate your own fixed sash or double-hung windows.

The Victorian style window shown in Fig. 5–12 requires an opening size of $2\frac{9}{16}$ inches wide by $5\frac{1}{16}$ inches high. This window has movable sashes, both top and bottom. The trim is the same configuration as on the Victorian style door. The San Francisco Victorian style window shown in Fig. 5–13 requires an opening size of $2\frac{3}{4}$ inches wide by $7\frac{3}{4}$ inches high. Because of the extreme height of this window, it is best suited for houses with a floor-to-ceiling height of 11 inches or more. The ornate trim on this window matches the trim on the San Francisco Victorian style door. It is an operating type window with movable sashes. The

Fig. 5–12
Victorian style window

Fig. 5–13
San Francisco Victorian style
window

Fig. 5–14
Palladian style window (photo
courtesy of Houseworks, Inc.)

rounded window and the ornate trim of this window add a nostalgic charm to any miniature house.

The Palladian style window shown in Fig. 5–14 requires an opening size of $3\frac{1}{16}$ inches wide by $6\frac{13}{16}$ inches high. This operating window requires a high ceiling, and lends itself well to stained glass in the fan-shaped transom. On many actual homes, Palladian style doors and windows are used on the first level coupled with either a Victorian or Yorktown style on the second level. A Yorktown style window is shown in Fig. 5–15; it requires an opening size of $2\frac{9}{16}$ inches wide by $5\frac{1}{16}$ inches high. This window is also an operating window with movable sashes. The style of this window, with its dentil trim, permits it to be mixed with other styles in perfect harmony. Most of the windows shown here are also available in side-by-side, and double-window units. Additional styles and sizes are available for small attic windows.

A window that is often used for Colonial or Early American houses is the standard eight-light window shown in Fig. 5–16. This window is non-working, with built-in shutters; it is also available in a twelve-light version. The opening size is $2\frac{9}{16}$ inches wide by $5\frac{1}{16}$ inches high. The shutters can be painted a contrasting color to accent the window outline.

The significant feature in favor of purchasing ready-made windows is the time-saving element. When you consider the number of windows in a large house and the amount of time required to build that many, the time saved may be truly significant. You also do not need to own the expensive tools that would be necessary to produce the ornate trim required for some architectural styles. Ready-made units also eliminate the extensive lumber and glass inventory that would be necessary to produce the various types or styles of windows.

Size limitations are probably the most significant disadvantage of purchased windows. Most styles are limited to one size, with a few exceptions. Painting of pre-assembled working windows can sometimes cause problems, as there is sometimes not enough clearance between the sashes. This can be overcome, and a smoothly operating window obtained, by disassembling the window, lightly sanding the two sash units, and then painting. (Disassembling the unit requires that two glue joints be broken to remove the sash.) After painting, reassemble the window and glue the joints broken during disassembly. Buying working windows in the kit form will eliminate this problem also, but the selection of architectural styles is very limited in kit form.

Recently, a new type of window has become available; it has been specifically designed for the removal of the sash from the window and the removal of glass from the window sash. However, the sash is constructed as one piece, and therefore is not movable. Because this is such

Fig. 5–15
Yorktown style window

Fig. 5–16
*Colonial style window with shutters
(photo courtesy of Houseworks, Inc.)*

a recent innovation, the style selection of this type of window is very limited. It is hopeful that in the future, additional styles will be added and that this concept will also be incorporated into the double-sash operating windows.

Bay Windows

Bay windows are available in ready-made and kit form. The selection in style and size is understandably limited, (for any manufacturer to supply all the various styles and sizes of bay windows which ever existed would be impossible). Some of the windows could be modified to match another style of architecture if necessary.

One of the most popular styles is shown in Fig. 5–17. This unit requires an opening size of $6^{15}/_{16}$ inches wide by 5 inches high. Its straight, sloped roof style lends itself well to most house styles. The Americana bay window shown in Fig. 5–18 requires an opening of $6^{5}/_{16}$ inches wide by $5^{13}/_{16}$ inches high. This unit has an attractive curved roof, a trimmed base and contains a window seat. The slender Victorian bay window shown in Fig. 5–19 requires an opening of $3^{9}/_{16}$ inches wide by $5^{3}/_{8}$ inches high. This window adds charm to any Victorian or Queen Anne house. It has special

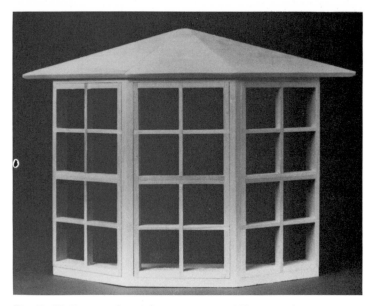

Fig. 5–17 Bay window (photo courtesy of Houseworks, Inc.)

Fig. 5–18
Americana bay window (photo
courtesy of Houseworks, Inc.)

Fig. 5–19
Victorian bay window (photo
courtesy of Houseworks, Inc.)

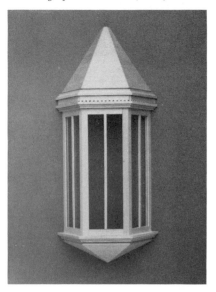

appeal when used on the stair landing, mid-way between the first and second levels of the house. When placed in this position, it permits the stairway to obtain some outside light and makes the staircase much more attractive.

Shutters

There are several attractive shutters available in a range of sizes. The assortment includes the paneled version, the raised panel version and the louvered panel version. Any of these styles will go well with any house style. They can be painted a contrasting color to emphasize the architectural style of the miniature house.

Several manufacturers produce the individual components for the louvered version and the raised panel version. By obtaining these individual components a miniature builder can design custom-made shutters of any desired size and style.

Etched glass

Several patterns and sizes exist in etched glass, for doors and windows. Individual window sections in rectangular, round and oval-shaped window panes can be used for either doors or windows. There are several recent additions to the available motifs in door panels, from roses to wildlife. These may not be available nationally, so check with your local supplier or mail order catalog. The door used on the Antique Store in Fig. 9–20 is a rose pattern, in frosted glass. Etched glass adds a distinctive touch to any house or store.

Stained glass

The stained glass that is currently available is a simulation in the form of a colored plastic decal that is attached to clear glass or clear plastic. It produces the effect of natural stained glass only with subdued or indirect lighting; a direct lighting is too strong and washes out the colors.

The imitation stained glass is available in a wide range of patterns and sizes, but limitations must be expected. One of its problems is the fact that it is noticeably an imitation. Standard cathedral glass is definitely too thick, so until a manufacturer produces a thinner cathedral glass, the plastic decal and colored plastic will remain the best available.

Staircases

The addition of a staircase adds a realistic touch to the appearance of the interior of the miniature house. Whether it is enclosed or open is generally established by personal preference. Construction of an open staircase requires more care because of its visibility; any mismatched detail is more conspicuous. However, open staircases are usually preferred because they generate an airy atmosphere that makes the room appear larger than it really is. Prefabricated staircases can be obtained to fit 8, 9, 9½ and 10-inch ceiling heights. Figs. 5–20 and 5–21 are examples of some of the available staircases, which come in a variety of styles: straight run, L-shaped, U-shaped and circular. Some units have hand rails, complete with newel posts. Select paneling is also available to finish the exposed area for a hand-crafted appearance. Most staircases are fabricated from basswood or pine, and can be stained to any desired color.

Considerable time can be saved by buying ready-made staircases. The amount of time required to do a layout of the stair, treads and risers, in

Fig. 5–20   (Left) Straight-run staircase (photo courtesy of Houseworks, Inc.)

Fig. 5–21   (Right) U-shaped staircase (photo courtesy of Houseworks, Inc.)

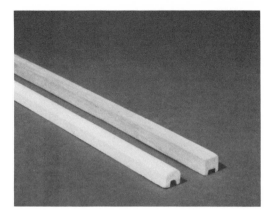

*Fig. 5–22
Staircase hand rail (photo
courtesy of Houseworks,
Inc.)*

addition to the actual construction, can be prohibitive. The stairs come in various sizes and styles. Widths range from 2½ to 3 inches.

Probably the most noticeable disadvantage to the ready-made staircases is the limited height range—between 8 and 10 inches. To utilize a higher ceiling requires modifying the existing staircase or constructing one from scratch. Individual components necessary to fabricate your own special design are available. In addition to the newel posts and balusters shown earlier, stair risers, treads and railings (Fig. 5–22) are also available in assorted widths.

Shingles

There are many shapes and styles of shingles available in wood, plastic and cardboard—regular, square-end shingles in cedar, redwood and pine, and fishscale, or half-round, in wood and cardboard. A diamond butt shingle made of cedar is shown in Fig. 5–23. Shingles made from cedar give an aged, weathered look of authenticity. The cardboard ones are generally not thick enough to add needed depth to a roof, but are exceptionally good for covering the side of a round tower or a curved surface, in addition to the house gable ends. There are also several styles of shingles that are available in tapered form, in which one end (butt end) is thicker than the other (top). This taper facilitates the shingling operation. The same thickness (nontapered) shingle must be modified or a noticeable gap will be generated between the first and second course of shingles.

Shingles are available in a variety of widths, from ⅜ inch to over 1 inch wide. While in reality some wood shingles are more than 12 inches wide,

*Fig. 5–23
Diamond butt shingle (photo
courtesy of Houseworks,
Inc.)*

I prefer to use the smaller size, about ¾ inch wide. The smaller shingles
make the house appear longer and generate a more pleasing proportion
to the size of the house. The cedar shingles of early vintage were 9 inches
wide, which is why the ¾-inch scale shingles appear to be more in
keeping with size than the more recent trend to a 12 inch width. Also
avoid the recently available thicker shingle if you want to be as authentic
as possible.

Asphalt shingles are also available in several styles; until recently the
choice of colors was limited to black, green, red and dark blue. Shingles
are currently available with a dash of mica to add to the reality. These
are available in square-end and scalloped-ends, and in strip form.

Serrated shingles or shakes are available in cedar and pine and can be
used for siding also. It is best to stain the wooden shingles prior to gluing
in place, because excess glue will prevent stain from penetrating the
shingle. The best method for bulk staining is to form a basket from
window screen or cheesecloth, and then dip in a container of stain, remove
and place on newspaper to dry (or remove excess stain with dry cloth).
When dry apply with glue to desired location.

The most significant advantage to ready-made shingles is the wide
selection of various styles, shapes and materials which are available. Next
would be the availability; most miniature specialty shops carry a wide
assortment, as do hobby and craft stores. Using the pre-cut shingles also

saves a certain amount of time over cutting your own. Some of the wood shingles are produced oversized, and this is very noticable on small roof areas. Be sure you stay in scale.

Siding

There are several styles of siding currently available for use in miniature house construction. Probably the most used and desired style is the clapboard style, which is available in three sizes: ¼, ⅜ and ½ inch (the spacing between laps or courses of siding). The ¼-inch spacing is equivalent to a 3-inch lap, which was used on Victorian and Queen Anne homes around the turn of the century, and other houses as well. The ⅜-inch spacing is equivalent to a 4½-inch lap, which was popular through the pre-war years. The ½-inch spacing is equivalent to a 6-inch lap, which was used up until the mid-1950's, when 9 and 12-inch shakes became popular. Let the vintage of your house decide on the size of siding used. The various sizes of siding are shown in Fig. 5–24, in descending order ¼, ⅜ and ½-inch. These sheets are ⅟₁₆ inch thick by 3½ inches wide by 22 inches long.

Novelty type siding, board-and-batten style and scribed sheathing are

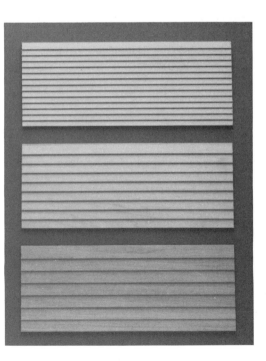

Fig. 5–24
Clapboard siding (photo
courtesy of Houseworks, Inc.)

also available in a complement of sizes to allow the miniature house builder a wide selection in the style and shape of the desired house.

The foremost advantage to sheet siding is the savings of time required to apply it. A large area can be covered in a short time. Alignment is also much easier because of the overlap from sheet to sheet, which automatically aligns each sheet.

However, sheet siding has a definite tendency to curl up whenever a coat of paint or glue is applied, so be prepared to deal with this problem. Also, the amount of scrap can become a considerable quantity if the miniature house has several gables to which the siding must be applied. The higher the gable, the more scrap that will be produced; the angle cuts for the sides of the gables cause waste.

Eave and Roof Brackets

Until recently the variety of roof brackets was limited to the Victorian style in a very small selection of sizes. The sizes and styles have now expanded to include porch brackets and gable-end decorations, but in many cases the builder will still have to fabricate custom brackets.

The ready-made eave brackets are a time saver in the construction of a miniature house. Some styles can save a considerable amount of tooling that would be required to produce the ornate trim. However, the number one disadvantage, currently, is the limited amount of variations in styles and sizes. At the present time the selection of available eave brackets is very limited. When a special design is required, the only alternative is to construct them from scratch.

Dormers

The dormers that are available today can be obtained in kit form or ready-made (Fig. 5–25). Yorktown and Victorian style windows are designed to fit the opening size of the dormer of $2\frac{9}{16}$ inches wide by $2\frac{15}{16}$ inches high. These dormers are designed for a 45° roof pitch, although they can be modified to fit any roof angle. Some are fabricated from soft woods, while others are made from plywood.

Wall and Floor Coverings

Clay Bricks

These genuine red bricks are available in sheets or individual bricks. The sheet forms are available in the common brick pattern or the "whole and half" pattern. There are also square patio bricks, in individual or sheet

Fig. 5–25
Dormer window kit (photo
courtesy of Houseworks,
Inc.)

form, which are especially attractive for an entrance alcove, foundations
and fireplaces. The clay has the feel of real brick.

The sheets have a flexible mesh backing, which permits the bricks to
be applied to slightly curved surfaces. Individual bricks can be cut with
a standard tile cutter, which allows assembly around square corners. The
sheets are six inches wide by twelve inches long and available only in
red brick color.

Plastic Bricks

Plastic bricks are produced in sheet form with an embossed brick design
or cut stone pattern. These are available in a neutral color only and require
painting to obtain the desired color. Most plastic glues or contact cement
will attach the plastic sheets to any desired surface. These panels can be
easily cut with scissors or knife. Once assembled and painted, they have
the appearance of real brick.

Wood Bricks

There are currently two types of wood bricks available for the miniature
builder. The predominate one is a silk-screened red brick design on a
wood sheet. The sheet measures $1/16$ inch thick by 4 inches wide by 22
inches long. These sheets can be obtained with the brick pattern running

either lengthwise or crosswise. The lengthwise pattern can be used for foundation walls, patio walls or a courtyard wall. The crosswise pattern can be used for either chimney stacks or pillar construction. The other type of wood bricks are individual bricks packaged 100 per package, and are manufactured from pine lumber. They can be painted any desired color, and are easily attached with any type of glue. Because they are cut individually, they must be installed one at a time. This can be time consuming, unless a straight edge is used to facilitate the application of the bricks.

Paper Bricks

Paper sheets of printed bricks are available in a selection of sizes ranging from a 6-inch-by-12-inch sheet up to a 17-inch-by-22-inch sheet. The colors vary from a light red to a dark tan. The inexpensive sheets do not have a matched pattern, and this presents some difficulty when attempting to cover an outside corner. The better quality sheets contain a nicely matched pattern and are a little more expensive. Although the paper sheets do not generate any depth to the bricks, they do indeed give the impression of a brick wall.

Wallpaper

The variety of miniature wallpaper patterns currently available is rapidly approaching the quantity and variety found in any large home decorating center. It is available in brick and board patterns, lattice, gingham, flower patterns, hearts, tulip patterns, lace, daisy patterns, squares and diamonds, in anything from the 8-inches-by-11-inches up to 17-inches-by-22-inches. Combinations of colors and patterns are endless.

Wallpaper designs of the 1750–1850 period have been faithfully reproduced for miniature rooms, houses and vignette boxes. This assortment of patterns is called the Tidewater Collection of Wallpapers, and is produced by X-Acto House of Miniatures Collectors Series. It is printed on quality paper to insure long-lasting color and ease of workability. Included also in this series are some colored outdoor scenes, to generate a panoramic view behind windows of shadow box rooms and vignette display boxes.

Some of the economy papers have pattern and color mismatch and therefore are difficult to mate at the room corners. To avoid this problem, have the pattern end at a door or window, and the mismatch will be concealed by the trim.

Wood Flooring

Tongue and groove flooring is comprised of 3½ inch wide sheets scored to resemble tongue-and-groove. The groove spacing is ⅛, 3⁄16, ¼,

⅜ and ½-inch, available in sheets that are 22 inches long. It is available in several different types of wood, in both softwood and hardwood.

Random width flooring is made up of strips of lumber cut to various widths and lengths. It is applied directly to the floor with glue as individual strips. It is available in several different types of woods, including pine, maple and basswood.

Parquet flooring is available in several patterns, with several of the more popular styles—parquet and basket weave—shown in Fig. 5–26.

Fig. 5–26   Parquet flooring (photo courtesy of Houseworks, Inc.)

They are generally produced in 2-inch-wide-by-6-inch-long sheets. Apply with a quick-drying glue or a contact cement.

Vinyl Tile

These are 1-inch square tiles on a 5-inch-by-10-inch strip with an adhesive back. Simply peel off the protective covering and press in place. These are available in black and white and are good for a kitchen or bathroom. There are also a variety of patterned sheets of vinyl in 12-inch-by-12-inch squares for wall or floor coverings, with a square pattern, a diamond shape, wood grain (in various colors), patterned gray slate and brick. Some of these are available in assorted colors also; check with your local supplier.

Terra Cotta Quarry Tile

This is real terra cotta, and it comes in individual ¾-inch square tiles. It requires mortar between the joints to give it a finished look. The mortar is available in a textured form, which can also be used as a stucco.

Rugs and Carpeting

Rugs add the finishing touch to any floor, and are available in an assortment of sizes, from a small 2-inch-by-3-inch throw rug up to a 13-inch-by-18-inch wall-to-wall carpet. You can buy every color of the rainbow short pile up to the deep pile shag rugs. Various rug kits are available in a hooked thread style, in a type completed with colored pens, or in needlepoint.

Fireplaces

Fireplaces can be obtained in brick, stone, plaster of paris, plastic, wood, metal and any combinations of these. Styles include Victorian Mantel, French Mantel, Spanish Adobe, Early American, Colonial and Italienate or Romanesque, to mention just a few. Some brick fireplaces are available in kit form, while others are produced in completed form only. Check with your local supplier. Figure 5–27 shows a brick fireplace in a Renovated English Antique Dollhouse by Mr. Dollhouse of The Dollhouse Factory, Lebanon, N.J.

Selection of styles is probably the most significant advantage in a ready-made fireplace. Styles exist in a range of sizes, from the small short unit to the complete walled unit. The variations in material are also an important feature. However, some units are built without regard to scale, with oversized bricks or stones and in some cases the mantel is completely out of proportion.

Fig. 5–27
Renovation of English
antique dollhouse. (photo
courtesy of Mr. Dollhouse)

Wiring

Wiring of a house permits the far corners of every room to be lighted, adding a special lived-in appearance. Systems for miniature house wirings are available from single lamps to complete circuits for every room in the house. Twelve volt transformers with a capacity of 35 light bulbs would permit two lights in each room of a 17-room house, and a security light by the front door. The miniature house described in later chapters has several areas available for a transformer to be installed. It can be located under the staircase, in the attic area, or behind the foundation. Several transformers and wiring systems could be included if more outlets are desired. Some systems use a thin tape which is easy to conceal behind wallpaper. In some systems, outlets and plugs are out-of-scale and can detract from your house.

Suppliers

Midwest Products Co.
400 South Indiana St.
Hobart, IN 46342
Wholesale only
Catalog $1.50

Northeastern Scale Models, Inc.
Box 425
Methuen, MA 01844
Wholesale only

Houseworks, Inc.
2388 Pleasantdale Rd.
Atlanta, GA 30340
Wholesale only
Catalog $1

X-Acto House of Miniatures
45–35 Van Dam Street
Long Island City, NY 11101
Wholesale only
Catalog of tools $2
Catalog of miniatures $2

The Dollhouse Factory
Box 456
157 Main Street
Lebanon, NJ 08833
Retail and wholesale catalog $2

6

DESIGNING YOUR MINIATURE HOUSE

Before you start collecting any specific data on a selected house, you should have a mental picture of what the miniature house will look like, when it is completed. There are many exterior details that are extremely attractive and therefore may be highly desirable as selected trim to be incorporated in the miniature house design. However, it requires a certain amount of self-discipline to refrain from adding an excessive amount of fine detail.

Proportion and style must be considered when the exterior trim is being selected. Not all features can be successfully incorporated into every miniature house. There are very few styles of house that are attractive with an excessive amount of ornate trim. The most adaptable style in this regard is the classic Victorian and even then an overabundance of ornate trim tends to be gaudy. The other style that has an extreme amount of stylized embellishments is the San Francisco Victorian. The facades in general and the entrances in particular on these stately structures are extravagantly adorned with elements from Italianate, Romanesque and Victorian architecture. This successful blend of styles is not found in any other prominent type of architecture.

In the United States there are some very distinct architectural styles that are peculiar to certain geographical areas. The Cape Cod house, the Salt Box and the original Colonial houses are indicative of the New England area, and more specifically the Boston and Cape Cod areas. The stately Southern Plantation house had its origin in the South and even today very few reproductions of this stylish house are found north of the Mason-Dixon line or west of the Mississippi River. The San Francisco Victorian can only be found in the Bay Area of San Francisco. There are very few styles of houses that are not restricted to a regional area. Among these few exceptions is the famous Victorian style, which has graced the entire landscape from the east coast to the west after being introduced into the upper Potomac and Chesapeake Bay area.

As a preface to establishing the exact architectural style for your miniature house, some specific features of particular homes have been included for your consideration. Some of these features are very common and typical of many American houses, while others have some exclusive trait that adorns a very limited number of houses. If the precise style of your miniature house has not yet been firmly established, consider some of these unique features which can be easily included into any style of miniature house. Many of the houses shown here were built around the turn of the century and they contain many intriguing architectural features.

House Details

The house in Fig. 6–1 has several unique features that would enhance the appearance of any miniature house. The front door is flanked by narrow windows, under a cantilevered roof; the two small protruding windows directly above the roof on the second story are indicative of windows located at the head of the stairs. The dormers have ornate trim and stylized windows; the half-moon window on the gable end and the unique, narrow four-paned bay window add distinctive touches.

The house in Fig. 6–2 contains several outstanding features that will challenge the miniature enthusiast: the combination of fieldstone masonry and the cantilevered second story, combined with the support brackets; the eave brackets on the third story dormers; the architectural treatment of the gable end and the distinctively styled windows located on all three stories. All are unique aspects of this particular house.

The charming architecture of the house in Fig. 6–3 contains an attractive styled sun porch on the second story, with window casing of Byzantine influence; an intricate window pattern on the third story; detailed eave brackets on the gable end and also on the porch roof; a peculiar window arrangement on the left side, midway between the first and second story (undoubtably located at the staircase landing); and a combination of porch columns and brownstone pillars on the frontal area.

The house in Fig. 6–4 has a special door arrangement that would greatly enhance any English tudor miniature house. Also note the window treatment, surrounded with the brick pattern, and the wrought iron railings to the front and side.

The gable end in Fig. 6–5 has a particular window arrangement that is not commonly found on English Tudors. The balcony railing is another example of customized architecture, and is a feature worth considering.

The ornate gable trim in Fig. 6–6 contains delicate spindles coupled with open fretwork that truly makes the appearance of the gable an outstanding feature. The Victorian influence is exemplified by the fish-scale shingles located on the gable and also by the dentil trim used over the windows. The ornate roof support brackets for the bay window are shown in Fig. 6–7. Note the narrow lap of the clapboard siding, which is also indicative of the Victorian style.

The English Tudor house in Fig. 6–8 has an extraordinary trim detail on the upper story, along with the window style and arrangement. The cantilevered trim and the eave brackets between the second and third story are unique features on this particular house.

The house detail shown in Fig. 6–9 expounds the Victorian influence with the larger sized dentil trim located at the eave and the smaller sized

Fig. 6–1   House with interesting window details

Fig. 6–2   House with contrasting materials and unique architectural trim

Fig. 6–3   Byzantine-influenced window details

Fig. 6–4   Brick accents for doors and windows

Fig. 6–5   A unique gable end

Fig. 6–6 Ornate gable trim

Fig. 6–7 Ornate roof support brackets

Fig. 6–8   English Tudor trim detail

Fig. 6–9   Victorian dentil trim

dentil trim utilized on the dormer, roof eave and the porch trim. The curved bay section in the lower portion of the photograph is another attractive feature.

The impressive architecture of the house shown in Fig. 6–10 would be another candidate for consideration for the miniature builder, from the stylish dormer, eave brackets, roof brackets to the circular second story stained glass window. The unusual porch windows on the first story and the hand carved embellishment on top of the corner columns are fine examples of the Victorian style.

The English Tudor shown in Fig. 6–11 contains some noteworthy details peculiar to this specific structure. The protruding canopy for the entrance door is supported by brick columns and is the platform for a second story balcony. The roof pitch of the dormers are at a different angle than the roof pitch of the gable. The roof brackets on the dormers are exposed, whereas the roof brackets on the gable are covered and protected by the gable trim. The exterior trim on the body of the house is either vertical or horizontal, all angled pieces have been eliminated in this particular house. This is a departure from the typical English Tudor shown in Fig. 6–8.

The architectural features of the house shown in Fig. 6–12 are also unique to this particular house. The eliptical shaped stained glass window, the narrow clapboard siding, the columnar shaped trim flanking the dormer windows are all prime examples of individualized features being incorporated into the design.

The house in Fig. 6–13 has an unusual treatment of the dormer windows. The semi-circular facade pattern of the dormers is also utilized over the entrance to the house. The protruding brick wall section is a pleasing interruption to the normal rectangular box-shaped structure. This disruption of the vertical lines of the house gives the impression of a lower-than-normal height.

In the house in Fig. 6–14, there are numerous items that can be observed as unique features. The very narrow siding is one predominant feature; it also includes three short windows to the left of the door; interesting porch pillars and lattice work beneath the porch, in addition to massive roof supports.

The house in Fig. 6–15 contains several impressive features that make it an outstanding example of fine Colonial architecture. The striking shape of the dormers and the attractive windows located on the third story are impressive features that would accentuate the outward appeal of any miniature house. The windows on the first and second story are another significant feature displaying a different style with eight lights in the upper portion of the window and a single light on the lower half.

Fig. 6–10   House with unique window details

Fig. 6–11   Variation on the English Tudor

Fig. 6–12   House with stained-glass window

Fig. 6–13   House with semi-circular dormers

Fig. 6–14   House with unique porch details

Fig. 6–15   Typical Colonial house

The porch roof at the entrance door is capped with a wrought iron railing to form a second story balcony.

The house in Fig. 6–16 shows Italianate influence with the recessed arches above the first story windows. The railing located at the edge of the roof contains Romanesque-styled spindles that compliment the overall shape of the structure.

The house in Fig. 6–17 has all the makings of a fine miniature house, with the elaborate roof brackets, the window arrangement on the gable end, the modified bay window on the second story, the stylish front door and stoop.

Design Check Lists

The particular design of miniature house which was used in this book could easily be replaced by another model. There are many other styles of house designs that would have been suitable examples to use as an illustration for the purpose of generating the required floor plans. However, the particular features found in this miniature house provide some basic construction detail that can be utilized individually or in conjunction with other aspects in the construction of any miniature house. One prominent feature in this house is the use of angled walls in both the living room and the sun porch. The method used to construct these walls can be used in the construction of any basic bay window design.

There are many different approaches that can be taken to establish the basic design of the ultimate miniature house. A person can start by (1) selecting the exterior design of choice and then fabricating the interior room arrangement to accommodate the selected concept or, (2) establishing the exact floor plan desired and then generating the exterior design to fit that specific floor plan, or, (3) selecting an existing house and then building an exact replica of both the interior and exterior.

When you decide to build a miniature house and the selection process begins, so does an endless list of questions. What size will the house be? What shape of house will look the best? What style of architecture will be the most pleasing? How many windows and doors will the house have? Will the exterior be finished with siding or stucco? Will the roof be shingled? What color should the house be painted?

In order to resolve the decisions that will be required regarding the size of the individual rooms, the number of rooms and the relative location of each room, a check list has been prepared. To utilize this check list, start with the first column, which is identified as desired items, and make a check mark by the features you would want to include in your particular house.

Fig. 6–16   House with Italianate and Romanesque details

Fig. 6–17   Elaborate roof brackets and modified bay window

Then go through the list a second time, and identify the items that are required and must be included in the miniature house. If the two lists agree, then the items to be incorporated into the miniature house will have been established. If there is a discrepancy between the two lists, you must resolve which items will be included and which items will be eliminated. Once you have established the exact quantity and size of the individual rooms, you are then ready to design your specific house.

This check list was used to identify the features found in the forthcoming miniature house as an example of how to use the check list. The specific features you desire to be included in your own particular miniature house may vary considerably. The intent of this list is to reduce the number of undecided areas and establish a plan for determining what specific items will be included in the basic house plan. By utilizing the check list, you can readily determine the desired quantity of doors and windows that will be required to construct the desired miniature house. It will also identify the number of rooms on each floor plus the number of floors. This not only will help establish the interior room arrangement but also give an indication of the amount of material necessary to build the desired building.

The check list can be expanded to include a list of the quantity and size of the individual components, if that is desired. In this preliminary state it would be advisable to wait and determine the exact amount of components required after the desired size and shape of the miniature house have been firmly established. This list was designed to narrow the field of selection by the process of elimination. If an item on the list is not a desired feature, then exclude that item from consideration. Indicate on the check list only those features that are essential to the development of a specific floor plan. Then by reducing the list to the essential elements, the generation of the desired floor plan will be greatly expedited.

Floor Plans

To make the task of understanding the basic system of building a miniature replica more comprehensible, the miniature house shown in Figs. 6–18 and 6–19 was used to generate the working plans. The resulting dimensions were established to utilize available standard door and window components. Because of this, converting the actual dimensions to the scale equivalent is quite easy, which may or may not be the actual situation with the particular house style you select. However the methodology defined here will apply to any style house desired. The more complex the architectural design, the more detail that will be required. Generally the larger the house, the more rooms that it will contain and

Check List of Exterior Features

	DESIRED ITEMS	REQUIRED ITEMS
A. House style _Rural American_	x	x
B. Number of stories	2	2
C. Number of exterior doors	3	3
1. operating	3	3
2. non-operating		
D. Number of windows standard size	14	14
1. operating or non-operating	N.O.	N.O.
2. removable sash or fixed sash	R	R
E. Porch or stoop _Porch_	yes	yes
1. open	x	x
2. enclosed		
F. Balcony, veranda, sun porch _Sun Porch_	x	x
G. Exterior wall finish		
1. paint		
2. stucco		
3. shingles		
4. clapboard siding	x	x
5. batten strips		
H. Roof Style		
1. gambrel		
2. flat		
3. mansard		
4. gable	x	x
5. gothic		
6. flat		
I. Roof finish		
1. shingles	x	x
2. dormers		
3. attic access	x	x
J. Foundation (required with porch)	x	x
K. Special features		
1. shutters		
2. gutters		
3. chimney	x	x
4. bracket trim	x	x

Check List of Interior Features

	DESIRED ITEMS	REQUIRED ITEMS	1ST STORY	2ND STORY	ROOM SIZE AND REMARKS
A. Selection of rooms					
1. Kitchen	x	x	x		12 × 12
2. Dining room	x	x	x		12 × 16
3. Living room	x	x	x		11 × 16
4. Master bedroom	x	x		x	11 × 16
5. Bedroom	x	x		x	12 × 12
6. Bedroom					
7. Bathroom	x	x		x	8 × 9
8. Study or den					
9. Sewing room					
10. Hallway	x	x		x	8 × 12
11. Closets	x	x		x	2½ × 8
B. Floor-to-ceiling height each story	x	x	9½″	9″	6″ attic wall
C. Staircase	x	x			
1. open	?				
2. enclosed	?				
3. with landing	?				
D. Built-ins					
1. bookcases					
2. china closets					
3. fireplace	x	x	x		
4. bay window (porch)	x	x		x	
5. kitchen cabinets					
E. Interior doors					
1. operating	x	x			
2. non-operating					
3. number of doors	4	4		4	
F. Interior decorating (list specific room)					
1. baseboard molding	all	all	x	x	
2. chair rail molding	x	x	Kit D.R.		
3. paneling					
4. wallpaper	x	x			
G. Floor covering (list specific rooms)					
1. wood flooring	x	x	D.R.		
2. tile	x	x	Kit	Bath	
3. parquet					
4. rugs	x	x	Kit		
5. carpet	x	x	L.R.		
H. Lighting system	?	?			
1. ceiling fixtures					
2. wall outlets					
3. transformer					
4. number of lamps					

Fig. 6–18
Rural American miniature
house (front)

Fig. 6–19   Rural American
miniature house (back)

thus the larger quantity of floor plans, drawings and elevation views that will be required to obtain all the necessary dimensions. For the purposes of this section, we will assume you are making a replica of an existing house.

Once you have selected the style and size of the house you are going to build, the next step is to acquire all the pertinent data and dimensions to produce the working drawings. You don't have to be a registered architect or a licensed carpenter to understand the basic mathematics involved in the generation of floor plans, although some basic knowledge of construction principles and a certain amount of logic are highly desirable. Dollhouse construction is the same as any other subject, the more knowledge and information you can obtain on the subject the easier the task becomes.

The simplest method of producing a set of plans for a miniature replica of any house or building would be to acquire the actual blueprints from which original structure was built and reduce these dimensions to the $\frac{1}{12}$ scale. Where this is not possible, an option would be to obtain the services of an architectural draftsperson to prepare the necessary working drawings. That approach would require a significant cash outlay and eliminate the job of doing it yourself. The best recourse or alternative is to generate the required plans yourself. This is where the challenge begins.

Data Collection

In the process of establishing the actual dimensions and generating the required sketches, the system of dimensioning will run contrary to standard architectural practices, but we are trying to mentally dissect the structure to arrive at the necessary dimensions to make workable drawings, and eventually the desired plans. If the house you are going to build is several stories tall or contains an elaborate amount of oramental trim, a camera becomes a very useful tool in the collection of details for both the exterior and interior. A photo eliminates the possibility of the errors that often happen when you rely strictly on memory. Even the best of memories tend to overlook some of the more important details.

If the miniature house is to be built from photos, take several shots of each side of the house and any special features, such as bay windows, porches, fireplace chimneys and attic windows. These photos will also help establish the relative position between other significant features, such as doors and windows, and the first and second stories. Be sure to add a measuring device such as a yardstick or a board of a known length to indicate height or length. Make this device as conspicuous as possible, with the markings at foot intervals clearly marked. These photos must be taken directly facing the subject; otherwise the dimensions will become distorted. The amount of distortion will vary with the angle of camera to the subject. Freehand sketches can be substituted for the photos but when one considers the amount of time involved and the accuracy obtained, it is difficult to compete with a camera.

Unless the house is close to where you live, try to obtain all the pertinent data you need on the first trip. This is where the camera will be indispensible. If the house is a 6-hour drive away, it can be quite disturbing to discover when arriving home that you forgot to measure the length of the porch, or don't know whether the attic had a round window or a square one. With the photos in hand, all the guesswork is eliminated. With a yardstick or other measuring device, you can determine the height or length of various objects by merely scaling the actual photograph.

To organize all the collected data, dimensions, photos and sketches that will be required before the working drawings can be prepared, it is recommended that a looseleaf notebook or folder be used. Establish separate sections for Interior and Exterior. Subsections can provide space for each room and contain sketches and photos of significant details such as casing trim on doors, windows, staircases, bookcases, fireplaces and other built-ins. The exterior section can include the details and dimension for porches, details of stained glass windows, siding, shingles, and standard and ornate roof trim.

First-Story Floor Plans

To start your data collection, make a sketch of the entire first story and identify each room as shown in Fig. 6–20. Make the sketch to fit on a standard sheet of 8½ × 11 graph paper, with ¼-inch grids. Suggestion: let each square equal 2 feet actual dimension. To this sketch or drawing add the floor dimensions, length and width as indicated. In obtaining the actual dimensions whether interior or exterior, I strongly recommend two people—one to take the actual measurement, and one to record the dimensions on the sketch. It is very awkward for one individual to do both of these tasks at the same time.

Record all measurements in *actual* feet and inches to assure accuracy. Then convert the actual dimensions to the ¹⁄₁₂ scale directly adjacent to the sketch and actual dimensions. This will allow you a chance to cross-check for accuracy. For additional assurance of reducing error, record the dimension in feet and inches. A dimension of exactly "3 feet" should be recorded as 3'-0" and not as 3' or 36". The reason for this is that when you record it in either of the latter ways you cannot tell if a portion of the dimension has been omitted or not. By writing it as 3'-0" you are certain nothing has been left out. With the number of dimensions to be recorded,

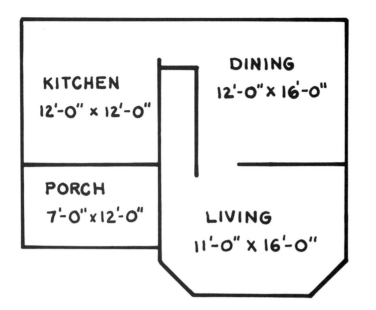

*Fig. 6–20
First floor plan*

it's a consoling thought to know you have not omitted a part of the dimension.

Kitchen

Now, make a sketch of each individual room, as shown in Fig. 6–21 for the kitchen. When making the sketches for individual rooms, use a scale of one square equals 1 foot on the ¼-inch grid graph paper, for more accuracy. On any given wall try to locate all features, doors and windows primarily, from the same starting point. If you decide to change the size or location of one feature later, it will not affect the remaining dimensions.

When any given sketch is completed add the dimension conversion table, shown in Fig. 6–22, adjacent to the respective floor plan sketch, and include all the dimensions you deem appropriate. Record the dimensions in an orderly manner and be consistent from room to room. Starting at the extreme lower left corner of the plan and working clockwise works well. Where you actually start does not matter, but being consistent does. Adding the overall room scale dimensions to the top of the conversion table is another helpful hint to reduce error. Add any personal notes or remarks to make the detail more explicit.

Next make detailed sketches of any individual walls that contain significant features; detailing bare walls is a waste of time and energy. On walls that contain intricate detail a photograph may be warranted, be sure

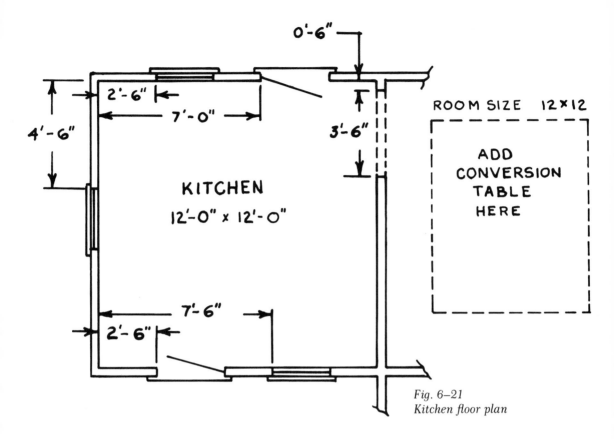

Fig. 6–21
Kitchen floor plan

Fig. 6–22
Dimension conversion table

ROOM SIZE   12 × 12

ACTUAL TO SCALE	
2'- 6"	$2\frac{1}{2}$
7'- 6"	$7\frac{1}{2}$
4'- 6"	$4\frac{1}{2}$
2'- 6"	$2\frac{1}{2}$
7'- 0"	7
0'- 6"	$\frac{1}{2}$
3'- 6"	$3\frac{1}{2}$

to include a measuring device, so dimensions can be obtained later. The first elevation view of a kitchen wall is the exterior kitchen wall, which contains the appropriate dimensions for the window location. Fig. 6–23 details the exterior kitchen wall and does not have the window opening size listed; insert the dimensions of the appropriate style and size selected from the component section. Then complete the conversion table with the necessary dimensions. Then proceed to the next wall, which is the kitchen back wall and make the necessary sketch (Fig. 6–24). After establishing the appropriate dimensions add the conversion table as indicated. (Note: the door knob can be utilized to indicate direction of door opening.)

Proceeding in a clockwise direction, the next wall to consider is the common wall between kitchen and stairwell. The detail of the kitchen side of the common kitchen/dining room wall is shown in Fig. 6–25. Again complete the conversion table. It would be appropriate here to include sketches of any significant features such as built-in cupboards or china cabinets. Include sufficient dimensions so that it can be constructed from the sketch.

Next, proceed to the remaining wall and detail the kitchen front wall as shown in Fig. 6–26. Include the appropriate size of openings for the selected door and window style, then complete the dimension conversion table as shown.

Dining Room

Proceed with the dining room in the same manner as with the kitchen. First, make a sketch of the overall room layout. The floor plan for the dining room is shown in Fig. 6–27. Then proceed to make appropriate drawings of the individual walls. Start by making the elevation view of the stairwell wall as shown in Fig. 6–28, and include the dimension conversion table. Normally the next step would be to proceed with the exterior wall, but because the windows are located at the same floor-to-window-sill dimensions and are the same height as in the kitchen, this view can be bypassed. The appropriate wall location of these windows can be determined from the dining room floor plan. (If the windows had been of different width or heights the sketch would have been included). The next wall to be sketched is the common dining room/living room wall as shown in Fig. 6–29. (The basement access door can be added if desired, beneath the staircase, and this space used for a closet.)

Living Room

Proceed to make an overall plan view of the living room and identify the special features as shown in Fig. 6–30. Then make a sketch or drawing

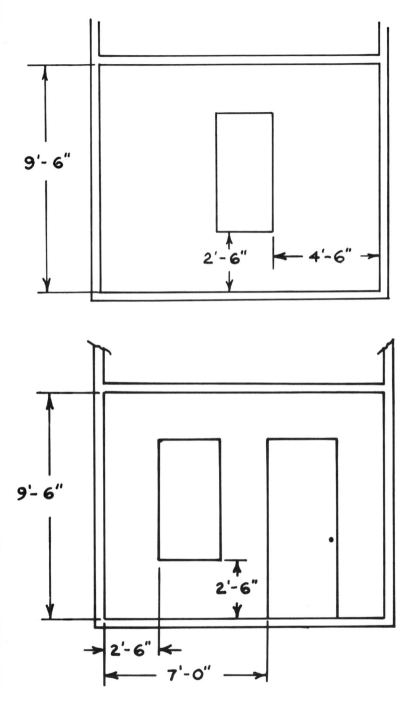

ACTUAL	SCALE
9'- 6"	$9\frac{1}{2}$
4'- 6"	$4\frac{1}{2}$
2'- 6"	$2\frac{1}{2}$

Fig. 6–23
Exterior kitchen wall

ACTUAL	SCALE
9'- 6"	$9\frac{1}{2}$
2'- 6"	$2\frac{1}{2}$
7'- 0"	7
2'- 6"	$2\frac{1}{2}$

Fig. 6–24
Back kitchen wall

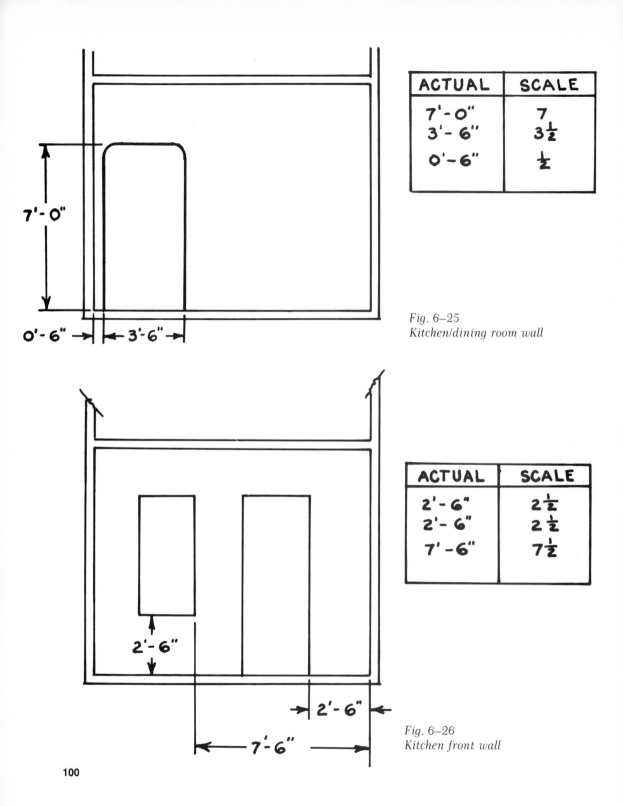

ACTUAL	SCALE
7'-0"	7
3'-6"	3½
0'-6"	½

Fig. 6–25
Kitchen/dining room wall

ACTUAL	SCALE
2'-6"	2½
2'-6"	2½
7'-6"	7½

Fig. 6–26
Kitchen front wall

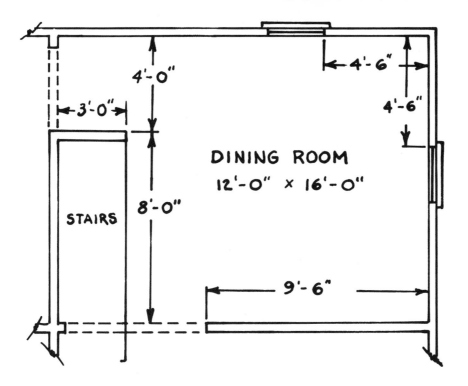

DINING ROOM
12'-0" × 16'-0"

STAIRS

4'-0"

3'-0"

4'-6"

4'-6"

8'-0"

9'-6"

Fig. 6–27
Dining room floor plan

ROOM SIZE 12 × 16

ACTUAL	SCALE
8'-0"	8
3'-0"	3
4'-0"	4
4'-6"	4 $\frac{1}{2}$
4'-6"	4 $\frac{1}{2}$
9'-6"	9 $\frac{1}{2}$

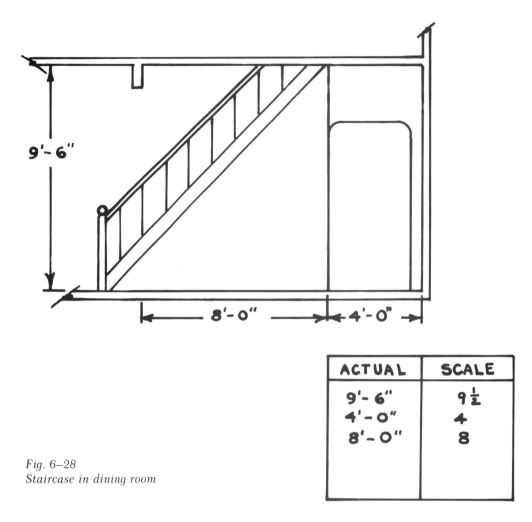

9'- 6"

8'- 0"   4'- 0"

ACTUAL	SCALE
9'- 6"	$9\frac{1}{2}$
4'- 0"	4
8'- 0"	8

Fig. 6–28
Staircase in dining room

of the living room wall on the porch side, showing door location and corner window section as shown in Fig. 6–31. Next sketch the archway located between the dining room and living room as shown in Fig. 6–32, including necessary dimensions. Proceed to the next wall and sketch the outside living room wall, as shown in Fig. 6–33; include the location of the angled wall.

Make a sketch or drawing of the living room exterior fireplace wall to show the detail of the fireplace, as shown in Fig. 6–34. Include all dimensions that seem appropriate, and the dimension conversion table. If the fireplace contains an extreme amount of detail, additional sketches

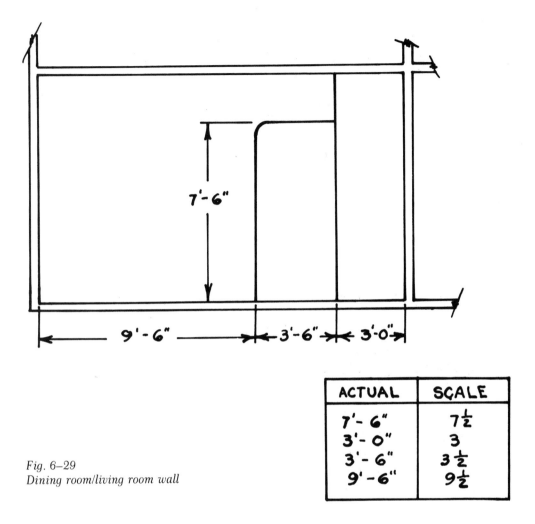

Fig. 6–29
Dining room/living room wall

ACTUAL	SCALE
7'- 6"	$7\frac{1}{2}$
3'- 0"	3
3'- 6"	$3\frac{1}{2}$
9'- 6"	$9\frac{1}{2}$

or photos may be prudent, with any necessary dimensions. Because of the common dimensions for window width and elevation as in the other rooms, separate sketches are not required. The relative positions of the windows and door can be obtained from the floor plan.

Porch
The size of the porch floor is 7'-0" × 12'-0" (7" × 12"). This is the only significant dimension that needs to be included in the overall plan layout at this time. Basically, this completes the necessary interior plan views

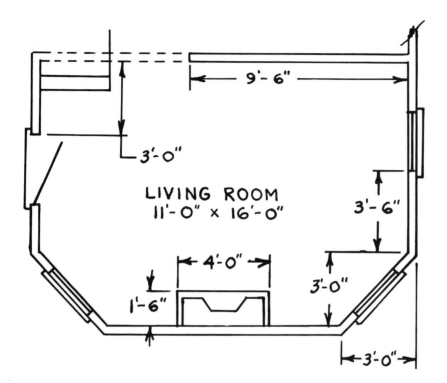

LIVING ROOM
11'-0" × 16'-0"

9'-6"

3'-0"

3'-6"

3'-0"

4'-0"

1'-6"

3'-0"

Fig. 6–30
Living room floor plan

ROOM SIZE   11 × 16

ACTUAL	SCALE
3'-0"	3
9'-6"	9½
3'-6"	3½
3'-0"	3
3'-0"	3
4'-0"	4
1'-6"	1½

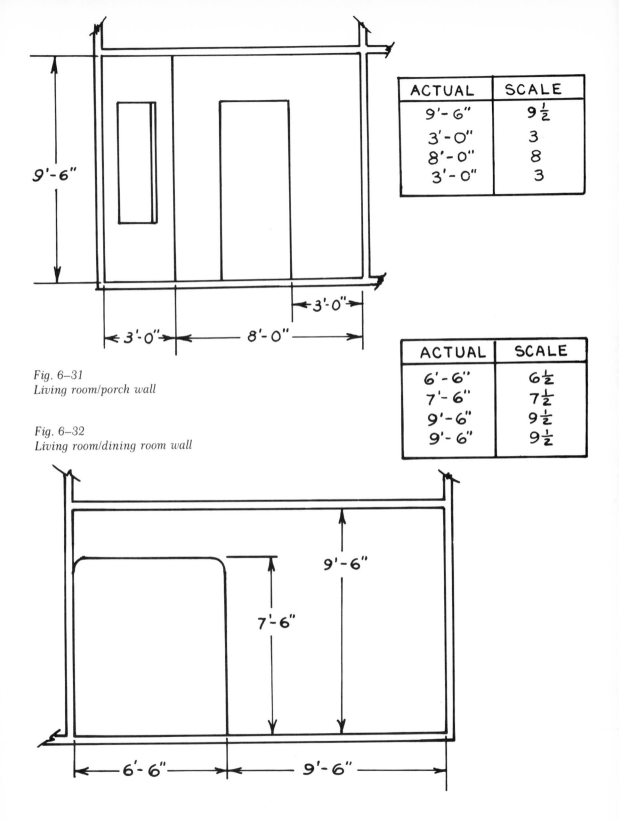

ACTUAL	SCALE
9'-6"	$9\frac{1}{2}$
3'-0"	3
8'-0"	8
3'-0"	3

Fig. 6–31
Living room/porch wall

ACTUAL	SCALE
6'-6"	$6\frac{1}{2}$
7'-6"	$7\frac{1}{2}$
9'-6"	$9\frac{1}{2}$
9'-6"	$9\frac{1}{2}$

Fig. 6–32
Living room/dining room wall

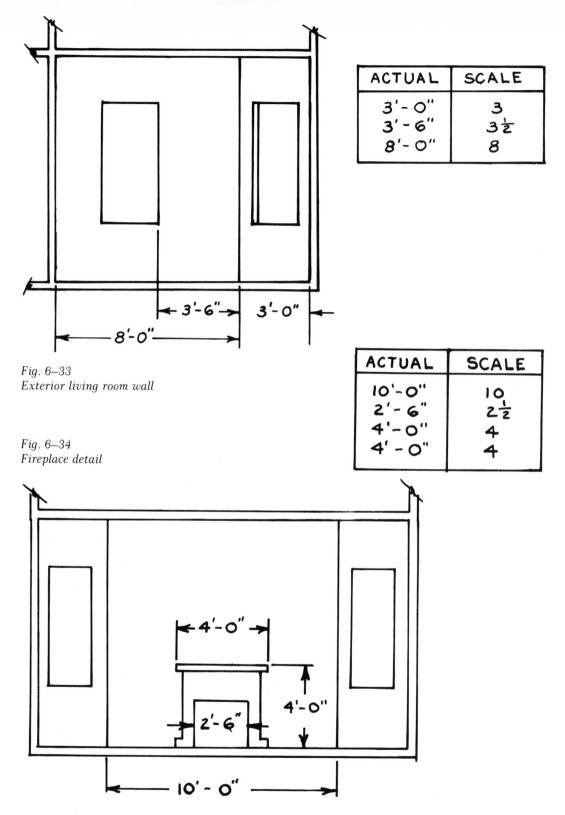

ACTUAL	SCALE
3'-0"	3
3'-6"	3½
8'-0"	8

Fig. 6–33
Exterior living room wall

Fig. 6–34
Fireplace detail

ACTUAL	SCALE
10'-0"	10
2'-6"	2½
4'-0"	4
4'-0"	4

and the elevation drawings of the first story. The porch detail will be covered as part of the exterior elevation detail.

Second Story Floor Plans

At the second level, continue the data accumulation, with the same procedure established for the first level. Make a floor plan sketch of the entire second floor, as shown in Fig. 6–35 identifying each room and overall dimensions. Then continue to make individual drawings of each room starting at the lower left side and continuing in a clockwise direction. The first area to consider is the sun porch.

Sun Porch

The floor plan for the sun porch is shown in Fig. 6–36. Add the proper dimensions and include the dimension conversion table. Then proceed to make the individual wall sketches as required. The detail of the center window wall section is shown in Fig. 6–37. Because all three window wall sections are identical only one sketch is required. (If the wall panel or window dimensions varied in size, additional drawings or sketches would be required.) The side walls do not require individual sketches because they are blank walls. This is sufficient detail of the sun porch at this time.

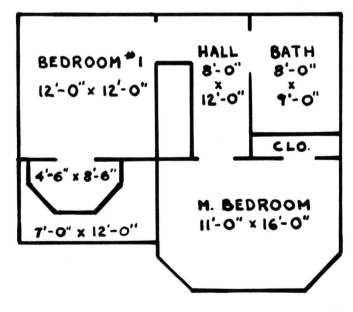

Fig. 6–35
Second-story floor plan

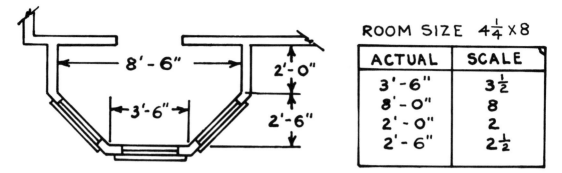

ROOM SIZE $4\frac{1}{4}$ X 8

ACTUAL	SCALE
3'-6"	$3\frac{1}{2}$
8'-0"	8
2'-0"	2
2'-6"	$2\frac{1}{2}$

Fig. 6–36   Sun porch floor plan

Bedroom

Sketch the bedroom floor plan as shown in Fig. 6–38, including the necessary location dimensions and the dimension conversion table. The first wall to be sketched is the exterior left-hand wall (Fig. 6–39). Include the location and opening dimensions as required, then add the dimension conversion table. (Note the change in the second story, floor-to-ceiling, height of 9 inches compared to the first story, floor to ceiling, height of 9½ inches).

Proceeding in a clockwise direction the next bedroom wall to consider is the exterior wall at the rear of the bedroom. Since the only feature on

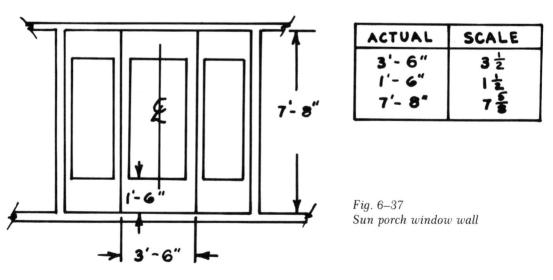

ACTUAL	SCALE
3'-6"	$3\frac{1}{2}$
1'-6"	$1\frac{1}{2}$
7'-8"	$7\frac{5}{8}$

Fig. 6–37
Sun porch window wall

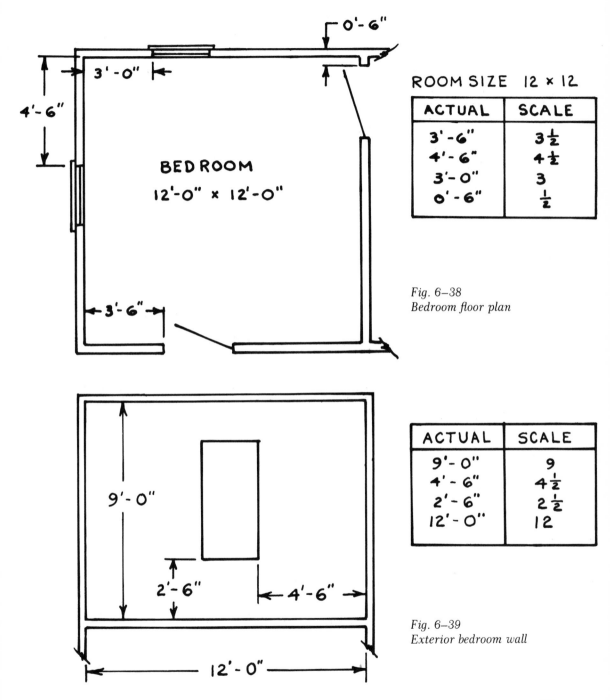

0'- 6"

3'- 0"

4'- 6"

BED ROOM
12'-0" × 12'-0"

3'- 6"

Fig. 6–38
Bedroom floor plan

ROOM SIZE 12 × 12

ACTUAL	SCALE
3'-6"	3½
4'-6"	4½
3'-0"	3
0'-6"	½

ACTUAL	SCALE
9'-0"	9
4'-6"	4½
2'-6"	2½
12'-0"	12

9'-0"

2'-6"

4'-6"

12'-0"

Fig. 6–39
Exterior bedroom wall

this wall is the window, and the floor-to-sill and window opening dimensions have already been established, it is not necessary to make a sketch of this wall. The bedroom floor plan can be used to obtain the window location dimensions when needed. However had this wall contained a significant feature like a fireplace or bookcase, a sketch would be warranted. The next bedroom interior wall, or partition, to consider is the common partition between bedroom and staircase. This wall is shown in Fig. 6–40; be sure to include dimensions and complete the dimension conversion table.

The next bedroom wall to be drawn is the common wall between the bedroom and the sun porch. Because of the commonality of floor-to-ceiling height, length of wall, and dimensions with other walls, this one need not be detailed. The door location can be obtained from the bedroom floor plan. If this wall contained some unique feature, then an appropriate sketch with dimensions would be included.

Hallway, Bath and Closet

This area was considered as a single item because of the commonality with the first story dining room dimensions. You can however, identify these as separate items if you desire. In normal circumstances they will not have the commonality with the first story and should be detailed separately. Detail the combined area of hallway, bath and closet as shown in the floor plan in Fig. 6–41. Include the necessary dimensions and

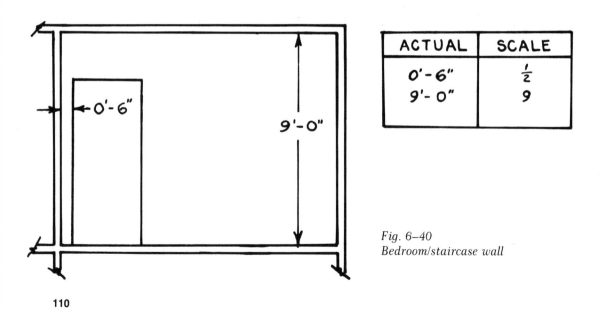

ACTUAL	SCALE
0'-6"	$\frac{1}{2}$
9'-0"	9

Fig. 6–40
Bedroom/staircase wall

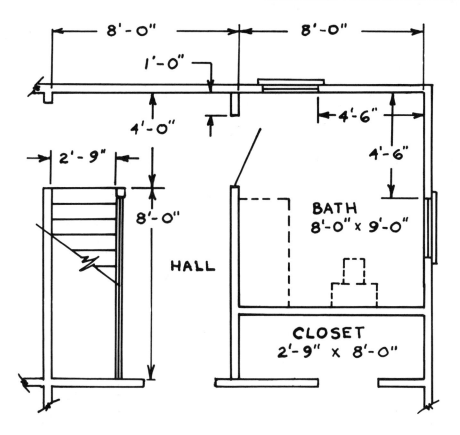

8'-0"

8'-0"

1'-0"

4'-0"

2'-9"

8'-0"

4'-6"

4'-6"

HALL

BATH
8'-0" x 9'-0"

CLOSET
2'-9" x 8'-0"

Fig. 6–41
Hall, bath and closet floor plan

ROOM SIZE 12 x 16

ACTUAL	SCALE
8'-0"	8
2'-9"	2 $\frac{3}{4}$
4'-0"	4
8'-0"	8
1'-0"	1
8'-0"	8
4'-6"	4 $\frac{1}{2}$
4'-6"	4 $\frac{1}{2}$

complete the dimension conversion chart. The arrangement and dimensions of the bathroom fixtures should be noted, if dimensions are taken from an actual house. Once the floor plan has been completed, then proceed to make the necessary elevation drawings. To start, make a drawing of the staircase partition as shown in Fig. 6–42. Define as much detail of the staircase railing as you think necessary. Include number of balusters and spacing, height of newel post, and configuration and height of railing.

Proceed to the exterior rear wall, common with hallway and bathroom. This wall does not contain any exceptional features so it need not be detailed. The window location can be obtained from the floor plan. The next wall to consider in the hallway area is the full length hallway wall common with the bathroom and closet. Because the door is the only feature on this wall, a sketch is not required. The door location can be obtained from the floor plan.

The next wall to consider is the bathroom exterior wall, with one window being the only significant feature; this wall will not require a sketch either. The window location can be determined from the floor plan. The next wall to consider would be the closet wall. Because this is a blank wall, no sketch is necessary.

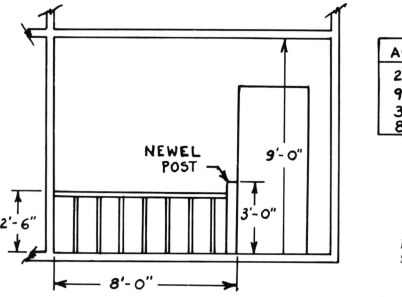

ACTUAL	SCALE
2'-6"	$2\frac{1}{2}$
9'-0"	9
3'-0"	3
8'-0"	8

NEWEL POST

9'-0"

3'-0"

2'-6"

8'-0"

Fig. 6–42
Staircase partition

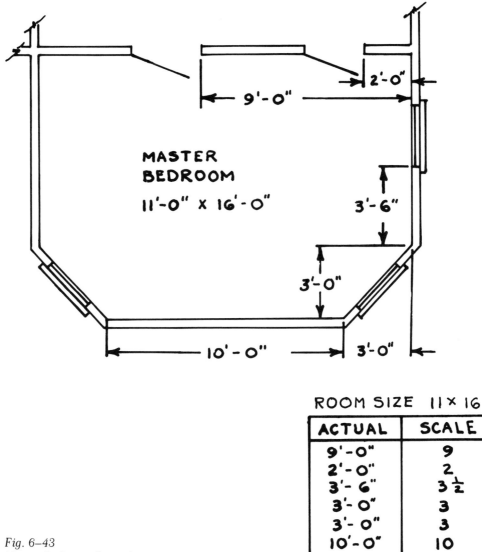

Fig. 6–43
Master bedroom floor plan

ROOM SIZE 11 × 16

ACTUAL	SCALE
9'-0"	9
2'-0"	2
3'-6"	3½
3'-0"	3
3'-0"	3
10'-0"	10

Master Bedroom

Complete the detailed floor plan for the master bedroom as shown in Fig. 6–43, and include the conversion table. Next, detail an elevation view of the partition to show the closet and bedroom doors, including the necessary opening dimensions to complete the drawing as shown in Fig.

6–44. The window walls are not included because of identical dimensions; in other cases they may be required. The location dimension for the windows can be obtained from the existing floor plan.

Porch Roof

The dimensions of the porch roof should be mentioned here, as it will become part of the second story floor plan. The dimensions are the same as for the porch floor, 7'-0" × 12'-0" (or 7" × 12"), not including the thickness of common walls, (1) between kitchen and (2) between living room.

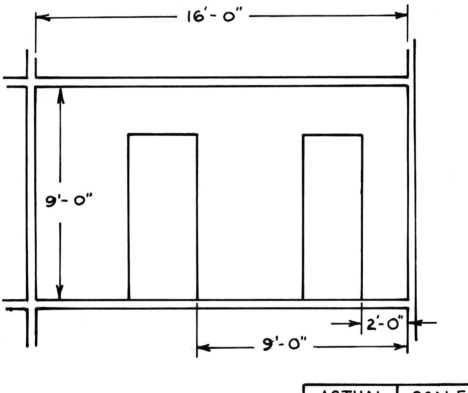

ACTUAL	SCALE
9'-0"	9
16'-0"	16
2'-0"	2
9'-0"	9

Fig. 6–44
Bedroom/hallway wall

Attic Area

If access to the attic is provided on the actual house, obtain as many dimensions as possible. These dimensions will facilitate establishing the height of the wall on the gable end of the house, location of the roof ridge and subsequently the roof pitch, all of which are necessary to produce the exterior configuration of the house. The dimensions that are essential include: (1) length and (2) width of the floor, especially if different than the second-story floor plan; (3) height from floor-to-ridge, and (4) side-wall height (height from attic floor to start of rafters, see Fig. 6–45); (5) number of windows, and (6) location of windows, (7) height of windows, and (8) width of windows. From Fig. 6–18 it should be noted that the corners of the attic are square, and not angled as on the first and second stories.

Obtaining the dimensions of the attic over the smaller bedroom will be limited to the length and width of the floor and the height of the roof ridge as shown in Fig. 6–46, because the walls terminate at the eaves. The width and length, both 12'-0" (or 12") will be the same dimension as for the bedroom floor and ceiling dimension. The ridge height measurement is 4'-0" or 4" scale.

This completes the amount of information that can be obtained from the interior of the house. The next area to be examined is the exterior detail to obtain as much of the remaining data possible to establish the pattern for the house.

Exterior Detail

With the amount of interior dimensions that have already been obtained, the majority of the remaining exterior dimensions will pertain to the architectural trim features. In any particular instance where inaccessible dimensions are required refer to Chapter 3 for various ways of obtaining close approximations. When starting with collecting data on the external features start at the ground level and work up. The first feature to be encountered is the height of the exposed foundation wall and the porch steps. Refer to Figs. 6–18 and 6–19, showing the porch and step detail.

Foundation

The height of the foundation wall can be determined by either measuring it directly or relying on the number of steps required to ascend to the porch landing. The front elevation drawings of the porch (Fig. 6–47 and 6–48) show that there are four step risers required (three steps plus the porch landing). Each step measures 0'-8" high, which means the di-

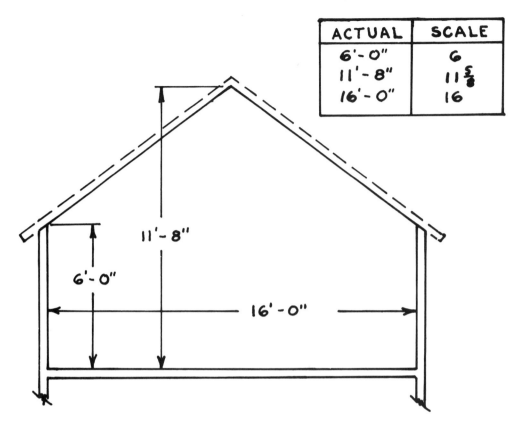

ACTUAL	SCALE
6'-0"	6
11'-8"	11$\frac{5}{8}$
16'-0"	16

Fig. 6–45
Attic over master bedroom

Fig. 6–46
Attic over small bedroom

ACTUAL	SCALE
4'-3"	4$\frac{1}{4}$
12'-0"	12

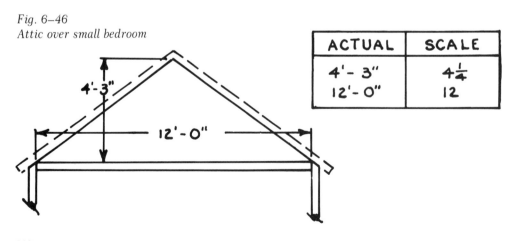

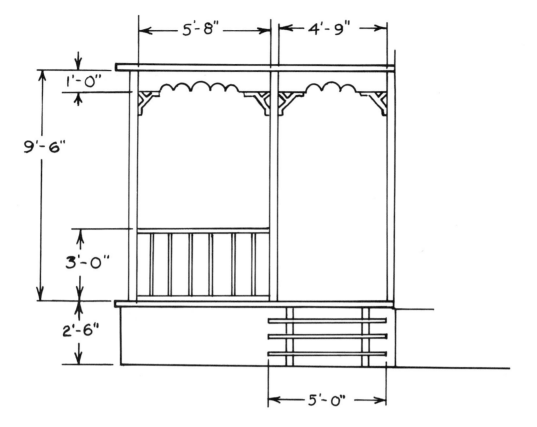

Fig. 6–47
Porch detail (front)

ACTUAL	SCALE
2'-6"	$2\frac{1}{2}$
3'-0"	3
9'-6"	$9\frac{1}{2}$
1'-0"	1
5'-8"	$5\frac{5}{8}$
4'-9"	$4\frac{3}{4}$
5'-0"	5

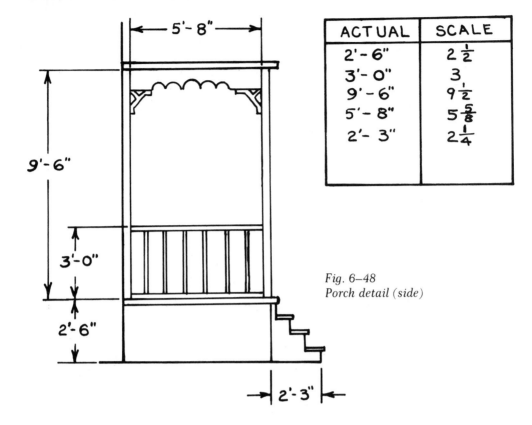

ACTUAL	SCALE
2'- 6"	$2\frac{1}{2}$
3'- 0"	3
9'- 6"	$9\frac{1}{2}$
5'- 8"	$5\frac{5}{8}$
2'- 3"	$2\frac{1}{4}$

Fig. 6–48
Porch detail (side)

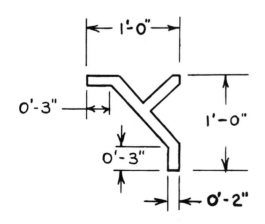

Fig. 6–49
Filigree detail

ACTUAL	SCALE
0'- 3"	$\frac{1}{4}$
1'- 0"	1
1'- 0"	1
0'- 2"	$\frac{5}{32}$
0'- 3"	$\frac{1}{4}$

mension required from the ground level to the top of the porch landing would be 2'-8" actual measurement or 2⅝ inch in scale.

Porch Detail

After completing the front elevation sketch of the porch in Fig. 6–47, proceed to make an elevation drawing of the side view of the porch as shown in Fig. 6–48. Make a note of the size and quantity of balusters required on front and side, also the number of porch pillars required. Then proceed to detail the filigree on the porch and other trim as shown in Fig. 6–49. Here is another instance where a camera would be useful. Include a measuring device in photo.

The next detail to consider is the rim on the top of the sun porch, detailed in Fig. 6–50. This feature is so small in comparison to other features that it is difficult to approximate. The comparison method is probably the best method to use to obtain a close approximation of the actual measurement if it is impossible to measure (Compare the height of the railing to the height of a known feature, like the height of a course of siding or the height of the fascia board on the eave of the roof, or the width of the window casing.)

Chimney

The next item to consider is the chimney. Because of its extreme height the best method to employ (next to the actual measurement) is the projection method explained in Chapter 3. Using this method, you will find that height is approximately 37 feet (actual dimension). The remaining dimensions can be obtained by actually measuring them (Fig. 6–51).

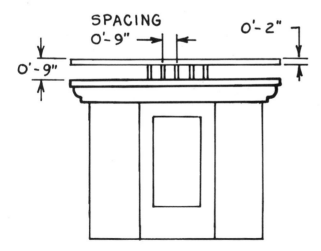

ACTUAL	SCALE
0'-9"	$\frac{3}{4}$
0'-9"	$\frac{3}{4}$
0'-2"	$\frac{5}{32}$

Fig. 6–50
Sun porch trim

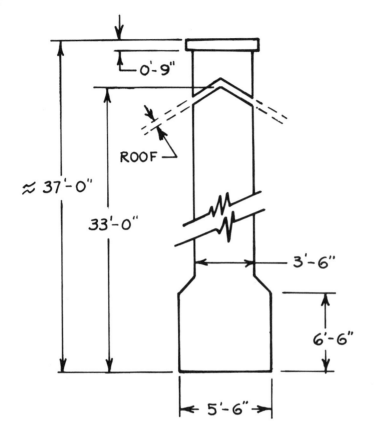

ACTUAL	SCALE
37'-0"	37
33'-0"	33
0'-9"	$\frac{3}{4}$
3'-6"	$3\frac{1}{2}$
6'-6"	$6\frac{1}{2}$
5'-6"	$5\frac{1}{2}$

Fig. 6–51
Chimney detail

Exterior Trim

The first feature to consider is the filigree trim on the master bedroom windows. These dimensions can sometimes be obtained from the inside of the bedroom, but if these dimensions are not easily obtained, then rely on the comparison method to establish a close approximation. The length of the protrusion over the window is approximately 3 feet (established from the inside, floor dimensions); the outside dimension will be slightly larger due to wall thickness. The filigree is approximately one half of the total overhang. It would therefore approximate 1½ feet in length. It also appears to be as high as it is wide, therefore the approximate height would be 1½ feet also. This should be sufficient information to generate a sketch or drawing of the trim bracket as shown in Fig. 6–52.

At this point, sufficient data has been accumulated to start consolidating the dimensions to establish the pattern for the individual parts

Fig. 6–52
Filigree detail

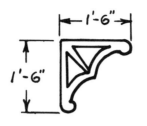

ACTUAL	SCALE
1'- 6"	1 $\frac{1}{2}$
1'- 6"	1 $\frac{1}{2}$

and then construct the miniature house. There are two remaining features that need to be defined before the house can be completely assembled. These features are (1) the height of overlap of one course of clapboard siding and (2) the width of the corner caps or trim. (The actual dimensions for these components are better established at the assembly level.)

The clapboard siding is 1/16 inch thick and available in 1/4, 3/8 and 1/2-inch spacing. The one selected for this house was the 3/8-inch spacing. Although either of the remaining sizes would be satisfactory, it may be a matter of availability and personal preference. However if the siding used is one of the other spacings, consider changing the corner cap width to maintain an appropriate proportion between the width of the corner caps and the height of the siding. The siding was applied flush to the door and window openings, before the components were installed. The trim used for corner caps and gable is 1/8 inch thick.

For the square corners of the house, the width of the corner caps were 5/16 and 7/16 inch. The 7/16-inch piece overlaps the 5/16-inch, to form a corner cap measuring 7/16 inch in both directions. For the angled walls on the living room/master bedroom, a 5/16-inch corner cap was used and beveled to match the adjoining wall. For the angled wall on the sun porch, the 7/16-inch corner bracket was used. This permitted the window casing to fit over the corner cap, thus giving more depth to the window casing.

7
PATTERN-MAKING

There are many ways to establish a pattern for the basic dollhouse structure and its individual components. The illustration of the miniature house in Fig. 7–1 is one of the various methods.

This particular house was designed with angled walls in the living room, bedroom and the sun porch, so that the builder can gain experience and confidence in building the angled walls. The experience gained here will be extremely useful in constructing bay windows or other angled walls for other miniature house projects. The construction of this house could be greatly simplified by merely squaring the corners of the living room and the master bedroom. It would eliminate some of the bevel cuts, but it would also eliminate part of the charm of this dollhouse.

Another alternate construction would be to assemble the porch as a separate assembly. This would permit the exterior wall of the kitchen and bedroom to be constructed as one piece, rather than as separate parts as they are here. Then the attic wall/living room exterior wall could be constructed as one piece also. The interior partitions could be built in a different arrangement also.

Once all the pertinent data and dimensions have been obtained and the necessary sketches, drawings and photographs have been completed, it is appropriate to start generating the patterns for the individual pieces. The more detailed and explicit the original sketches were, the easier this task will be.

Start the pattern layouts on ¼-inch grid graph paper, with any reasonable scale. Allowing each ¼-inch square to equal 2 inches is a good working size, to permit adequate space for the inclusion of the necessary dimensions. The scale of 1 inch per square can also be used, but the

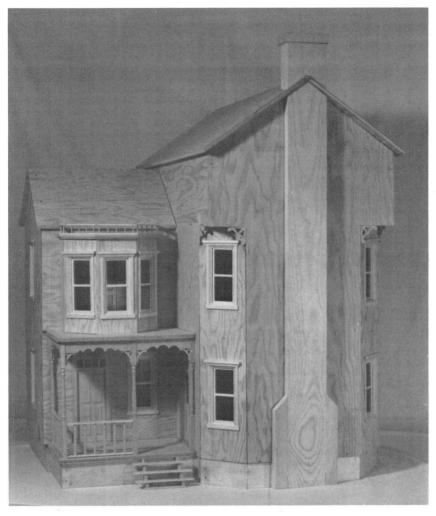

Fig. 7–1   Dollhouse (front view)

space for locating the external dimensions will be much more restricted. However, using the latter scale will increase the degree of accuracy that can be attained. Use whatever scale is the most confortable, but try and maintain the same scale from part to part. This will permit a better visualization of the structure as additional parts are defined and detailed. Using several different scales at the same time will only add confusion to the project.

The basic dollhouse was constructed from ⅜-inch plywood, including all floors, walls, partitions and roof sections. If a different thickness of plywood is used in the construction of the dollhouse, the dimensions determined here will have to be adjusted to compensate for the difference.

Pattern Basics

Several items will have an effect on the methods and therefore the outcome of the miniature house construction, and must be addressed and resolved before the patterns for the individual pieces can be finalized.

A concept of construction of the overall house must be determined before attempting to finalize the individual dimensions. Establishing the dimensions for one method of construction, and then changing the approach would require extensive dimensional changes, generally with catastrophic results. Devote a certain amount of time to considering alternate methods of construction and avoid the confusion. Several construction methods can be employed and developed to arrive at the completed house shown in Fig. 7–2. Generally the approach has been to build an enclosed box structure with the exterior walls attached to the required floor plans and then to add the necessary interior partitions.

The concept used to construct this particular house has been often considered by me but never put into actual practice until now. (A change in the method of constructing an L-shaped house.) An exterior wall and an interior partition are combined to form a single unit rather than two separate pieces. This construction is shown in Fig. 7–3, for the first and second stories of the miniature house.

Allowance must be made for the inclusion of the exterior walls and interior partitions. The interior dimensions as defined do not allow for the wall or partition thickness, they must be adjusted to include this thickness (Fig. 7–4). How and where these wall thicknesses are included is up to the discretion of the builder. If an exterior wall is the same width as the corresponding floor plan, then the adjacent wall length must be increased to include the wall thickness.

You must determine how access will be provided to the interior of the miniature house. There are several ways this can be accomplished. A wall can be removed and the side of the house left open, one or more walls can be hinged, or the whole house can be hinged in the middle to form two separate parts. In this house, access is provided through the open back, and through a hinged panel on the master bedroom/living room wall (Fig. 7–5). This access panel location may be changed to accomodate individual preference, but the dimensions and the required clearance should be carefully checked beforehand so the proper adjustments can be made. Calculating the dimensions for the components

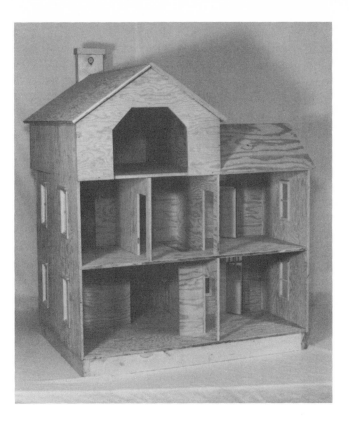

Fig. 7–2
Dollhouse (back view)

Fig. 7–3
Interior partitions of
dollhouse

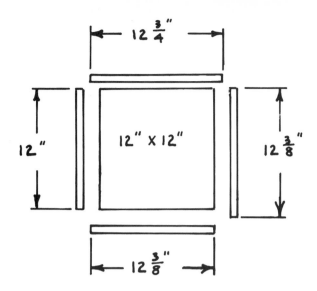

12 3/4"

12" X 12"

12"

12 3/8"

12 3/8"

Fig. 7–4
Wall thickness must be included in dimensions

Fig. 7–5
Hinged access wall

should be done with the *scaled* dimensions and not the full-size dimensions.

The building components used in the construction of this house were commercially available components. Therefore the opening cutout dimensions will be identical for all similar components, like exterior doors, interior doors, and windows. Openings for the windows are 3⁹⁄₁₆ inches wide by 5¹⁄₁₆ inches high; the exterior doors are 3¹⁄₁₆ inches wide by 7⁹⁄₁₆ inches high. Openings for the interior doors are 3¹⁄₁₆ inches wide and 7¹⁄₁₆ inches high. The dimensions of the openings are not marked on the patterns. Chapter 5 on building components describes many of the available doors and windows.

To establish the total length and width of the floor plan for any single story in the house, the overall dimensions of all the rooms located on that story must be considered. Unless the house is exceptionally large or complicated, this is not a major undertaking. The task of retrieving the desired dimensions has been greatly simplified by locating the overall room dimensions at the top of the conversion chart for each room.

First-Story Pattern

In order to establish the length and width of this floor, the dimensions of the porch, kitchen, dining room and the living room will be required. Here again the starting point and the direction to establish the desired overall dimension is not important, but because the kitchen was the starting point for the data accumulation, it will be used as the starting point for establishing the necessary dimensions for the first story.

To establish the length across the back of the house, the combined lengths of the kitchen and dining room are used; refer to the first story floor plan in Fig. 6–20 for the overall layout. The dimensions from the kitchen floor plan in Fig. 6–21 and the dining room floor plan in Fig. 6–27 are required. The dimensions of the respective rooms did not include the thickness of the interior partitions. Therefore, you must add ⅜ inches to the room lengths, for a total length of 28⅜ inches.

To establish the width of the house, refer to the first story floor plan in Fig. 6–20 for the dimensions of the porch and the kitchen floor plan in Fig. 6–21 for the dimensions of the kitchen. Add these plus ⅜-inch common wall thickness for a width of 19⅜ inches.

To establish the width of the house on the dining room side, refer to the dining room floor plan in Fig. 6–27 for the dimensions of the dining room, and Fig. 6–30 for the living room dimensions. For this house, these dimensions plus ⅜-inch common wall thickness equals 23⅜ inches wide.

The length of the house across the front of the living room is equal to

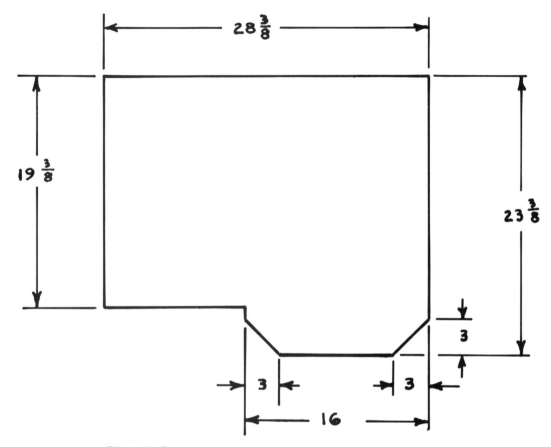

Fig. 7–6   First story pattern

the length of the living room or 16 inches, and is located 4 inches forward of the porch. This dimension is established by the difference between the widths of the sides of the house. Remember to show the corners of the living room angled 45 degrees or 3 inches each way. These dimensions are used to generate the first story pattern shown in Fig. 7–6.

Second-Story Pattern

To determine the dimensions of the second story, refer to the floor plan in Fig. 6–35, and note the individual room dimensions. It should be noted that in order to establish the length and the width of the second story of the house, the dimensions of the porch, bedroom, hallway, bathroom, closet and master bedroom are required.

To establish the dimensions across the back of the house, second story, refer to the bedroom floor plan in Fig. 6–38 and the hallway/bathroom floor plan in Fig. 6–41 for the required dimensions. The bedroom, hall and bath, plus ⅜-inch common wall gives a length of 28⅜ inches.

To establish the width of the house across the bedroom and the porch, refer to the floor plan for the bedroom in Fig. 6–38 and the second story floor plan in Fig. 6–35 for the necessary dimensions. Adding the figures, plus ⅜-inch common wall gives 19⅜ inches.

To establish the width of the house on the bathroom and master bedroom side, refer to the floor plan of the hallway/bathroom in Fig. 6–41 and the floor plan of the master bedroom in Fig. 6–43 for dimensions. Adding these figures, plus ⅜-inch common wall, will establish the width of the house on the bathroom/master bedroom side at 23⅜ inches.

The length of the house on the second story across the front of the master bedroom is equal to the length of the master bedroom, or 16 inches, and is located 4 inches forward of the porch. Remember to show the corners of the master bedroom angled for 3 inches each way or 45 degrees.

Draw the outline of the second story pattern as shown in Fig. 7–7. To this layout, the stairwell opening must be added. Refer to the second story hallway floor plan in Fig. 6–41 and locate the top of the stairs 4 inches (4'-0") from the back wall, the opening is 8 inches (8'-0") long and 2¾ inches (2'-9") wide. Because the stairwell is located from the bedroom wall, it should be measured from the bedroom side of the floor plan. To determine this dimension, take the length of the bedroom at 12 inches and add the wall thickness of ⅜ inch for a total of 12⅜ inches, for a location dimension. Position the stairwell opening with these dimensions and square with the side and back of the floor plan.

Third-Story Pattern

To establish the dimensions for the third story, which is the attic floor or the ceiling of the second story, utilize the same procedure as for establishing the dimensions of the previous two stories. The length across the back of the house is the same combination of bedroom dimensions and hallway/bathroom dimensions that were used for the second story to establish a total length of 28⅜ inches. The width of the attic floor over the bedroom area is limited to the bedroom width of 12 inches, because the porch area does not extend to the third story. Also, the wall thickness between the bedroom and the porch terminates at the third story and is therefore not considered in the width of this section. The width of the

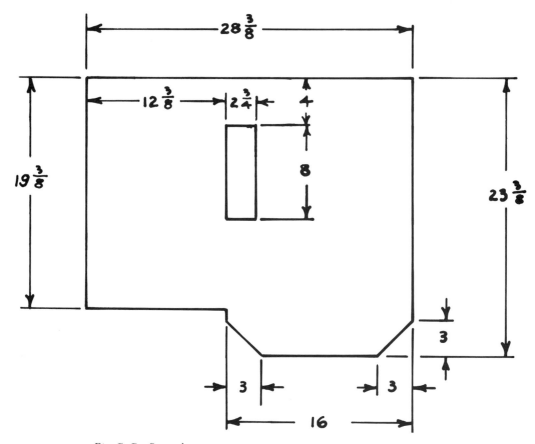

Fig. 7–7   Second story pattern

house in the hallway/bathroom and master bedroom is the same as the second story dimension of 23⅜ inches, except that the corner of the master bedroom is square and not angled at 45 degrees as is the second story. The length of the attic floor across the front of the master bedroom will be the same 16 inches and again the corner is square and not angled. With these dimensions the attic floor plan or the third story floor plan can be drawn as shown in Fig. 7–8.

With the required floor plans for the various stories completed, the next area to be considered is the exterior walls. Remember when establishing the height of the exterior walls, the thickness of the respective floors will

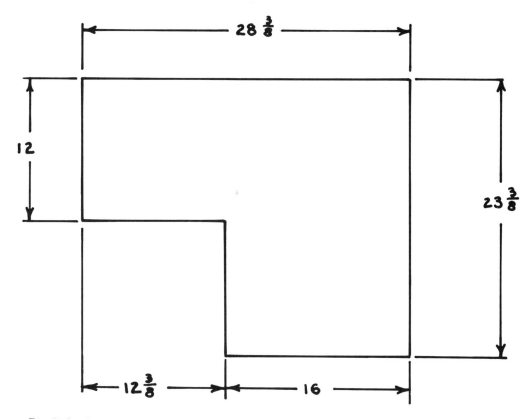

Fig. 7–8   Attic pattern

have to be added to the floor-to-ceiling heights, in addition to the attic clearance dimensions, when applicable.

Kitchen/Bedroom Gable Pattern

To establish the height of the kitchen/bedroom gable wall, refer to Fig. 6–23 for the first story floor-to-ceiling height, to Fig. 6–39 for the second story floor-to-ceiling height, and to Fig. 6–46 for the height of the attic dimension over the bedroom. Then, including the three floor thicknesses, the height of the kitchen/bedroom gable is found to equal 23⅞ inches.

To establish the width of the gable end, refer to the first story floor plan in Fig. 6–20; this width is limited to the width of the kitchen or 12 inches.

With these dimensions the kitchen gable outline can be established (Fig. 7–9). Next, locate the required window openings on the first and second story of the kitchen gable.

To establish the location of the window sill height in the kitchen, refer to Fig. 6–23. Adding on the floor thickness gives a sill height of 2⅞ inches. Note this dimension carefully, if all the windows are the same style and dimensions are the same, then this dimension of 2⅞ inches will apply to all first story window locations.

The horizontal position of the window can be determined from the kitchen floor plan (Fig. 6–21), which shows this dimension to be 4½ inches from the back of the house. With these dimensions the kitchen window can be located on the wall.

To establish the location of the window in the second story bedroom, refer to Fig. 6–23 for first story height, and to Fig. 6–39 for floor-to-window-sill height on second story. Adding these dimensions, plus ¾-inch (two floors) gives 12¾ inches. The horizontal position of the bedroom window can be determined from Fig. 6–39—4½ inches from the back

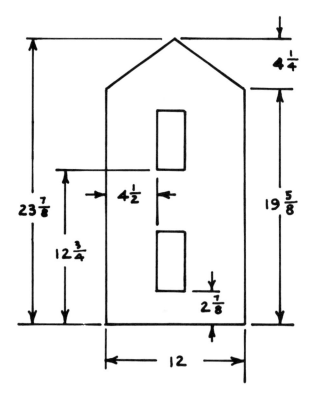

Fig. 7–9
Kitchen/bedroom gable pattern

of the house. Add these window location dimensions along with the required opening dimensions for the size of the window selected to Fig. 7–9. These dimensions complete the kitchen/bedroom gable pattern.

Dining Room/Living Room/Master Bedroom Wall Pattern

To establish the height of this exterior wall, refer to Fig. 6–32 for the living room floor-to-ceiling height, Fig. 6–44 for the master bedroom floor-to-ceiling height, and Fig. 6–45 for the attic wall height and the dimension from attic floor to roof ridge. By adding these dimensions together, plus three floor thicknesses, you get a height of 25⅝ inches.

The length of the dining room/living room wall at the eave is established by the length of the attic floor plan in Fig. 7–8, for a total length of 23⅜ inches. This dimension will apply between the roof eave and the bottom of the attic floor, or 6⅜ inches (this dimension is established by the height of the attic wall of 6 inches plus the attic floor thickness of ⅜ inch).

The length of this wall along the foundation will be determined by the length of the first story, from the back of the house to the corner of the angled wall in the living room, which is 20⅜ inches. However, this dimension must be increased by 5/32 inch to compensate for the bevel cut that is required to match the angle of the adjoining wall, thus making the total length at the foundation 20¹⁷/₃₂ inches. These dimensions will generate the outline pattern shown in Fig. 7–10. To this drawing add the required bevel on the leading edge of the pattern.

Window Locations

Refer to the floor plans of the individual rooms to establish the horizontal dimensions for the window locations. The vertical locations have already been established on the previous gable to be 2⅞ inches.

To locate the windows in the dining room and the living room on the first story, refer to the dining room floor plan (Fig. 6–27); the window is located at 4½ inches from the back wall of the house. Then refer to the living room floor plan (Fig. 6–30); note that the living room side window is located 3½ inches from the angled wall and that the angled wall is located 3 inches from the living room front wall. Therefore, the living room side window will be located 6½ inches from the front edge of the wall. Locate these positions on the first story end wall as shown in Fig. 7–10. Then include the window opening dimension for the selected style of window.

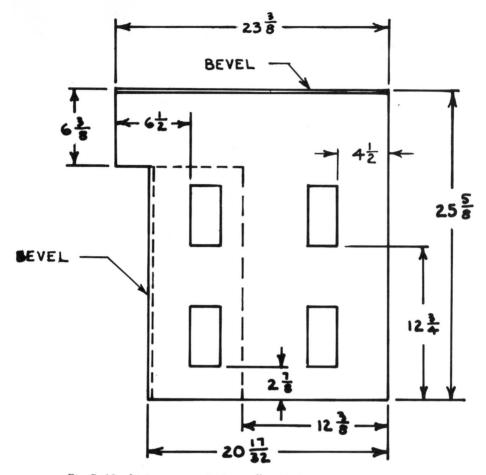

Fig. 7–10   Living room exterior wall pattern

To establish the locations of the windows on the second story, refer to Fig. 6–41 for the bathroom window location, and note this dimension to be 4½ inches from the back wall of the house. Then for the master bedroom side window location refer to the master bedroom floor plan in Fig. 6–43 and note the window is located 3½ inches from the corner angle and the angled wall is located 3 inches from the outside wall. Therefore, the window is located 6½ inches from the front edge of the master bedroom wall. The vertical locations for the windows have been previously established on the kitchen gable end to be 12¾ inches. The area defined by the dotted line is for a hinged wall section that will be identified later.

Front Gable Pattern

The front gable is comprised of the living room, master bedroom and the attic section on the front of the house. To establish the height of the front gable, refer to the living room wall view in Fig. 6–32 for the first story floor-to-ceiling height, the master bedroom wall in Fig. 6–44 for the second story floor-to-ceiling height, and the attic elevation drawing (Fig. 6–45) for the required dimensions. By adding these dimensions, plus three floor thicknesses, you determine a height of 31¼ inches.

To establish the width of the gable at the top, refer to the elevation view of the attic in Fig. 6–45, and note the inside width to be 16 inches. The overall width of the section will have to be increased by ⅜ inch on *each* side to compensate for the thicknesses of the two attic walls. Therefore, the width of the upper portion of the front gable will be 16¾ inches. This width will extend from the attic floor to the edge of the roof. The *inside* attic roof height, at the eaves, of 6 inches must be *reduced* to 5¾ inches at the extreme outside edge to compensate for the roof angle of 35 degrees. To this dimension (5¾ inches) the attic floor thickness of ⅜ inch is added to arrive at a total height of 6⅛ inches at the extreme outside edge of the side wall.

To establish the width of the front gable at the foundation, refer to the living room floor plan in Fig. 6–30. The total length of the living room is 16 inches. The two angled walls measure 3 inches each. Therefore, the width of the front gable will have an *inside* dimension of 10 inches. To this 10-inch dimension the ⁵⁄₃₂ allowance for each bevel cut must be added, so the total width of the front gable is 10⁵⁄₁₆ inches. Round this up to 10⅜ inches to allow for errors in cutting the bevels.

Next, determine the height of the narrow section, which is the distance from the foundation to the overhang above the master bedroom. By adding the two floor-to-ceiling heights, plus two floor thicknesses, gives 19¼ inches.

This is sufficient information to generate the pattern for the front wall gable as shown in Fig. 7–11.

Rear Gable Pattern

The gable at the rear end of the attic is identical to the top section of the front gable, as seen in Fig. 7–12. Because the dimensions were previously calculated for the front gable, it would be repetitious to do them again. The dotted line in the pattern shows the outline of the access opening to the attic. If the roof is to be hinged, this feature can be eliminated. To be considered will be the front wall section for the angled portion of the front wall for the master bedroom and the living room.

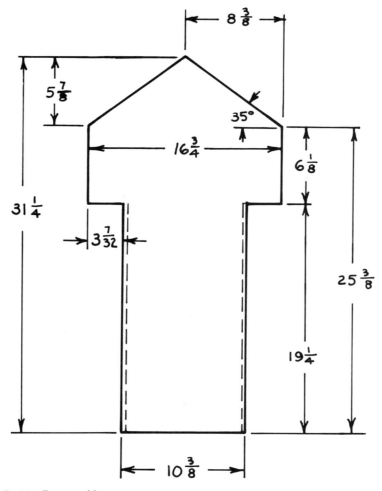

Fig. 7–11   Front gable pattern

Front Angled-Wall Pattern

Because this wall must mate with the lower portion of the front gable, previously defined, the overall height of this wall will be equal to the height of the lower portion of the front gable, or 19¼ inches.

To establish the width of this wall section, measure the length of this angled wall section on either the first story or second story floor pattern (Fig. 7–6 or 7–7). This dimension can also be calculated using trigonometry functions. In either case, the dimension will be 4¼ inches. To this dimension, the allowance for the bevel must be added to each side

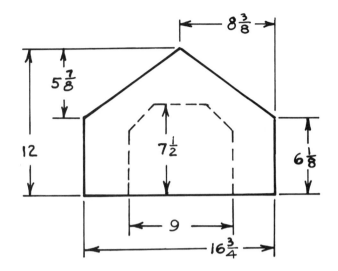

Fig. 7–12
Rear gable pattern

(⁵⁄₃₂), for a total width of 4⁹⁄₁₆ inches, (round up to 4⅝ inches to allow for trim).

The window locations have been previously defined for both the first and second story, so the pattern for the angled wall section can be drawn (Fig. 7–13). Include the required dimensions for the window openings

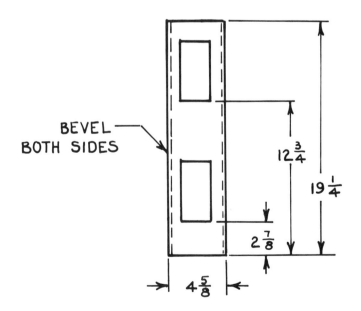

Fig. 7–13
Angled-wall pattern

and indicate the bevel on the sides. Two of these angled-wall sections are required.

Kitchen/Living Room Wall Pattern

To establish the length of the common wall of the kitchen and the living room, refer to the kitchen floor plan (Fig. 6–21) and the living room floor plan (Fig. 6–30). By adding the exterior kitchen wall thickness, the kitchen length, the interior partition thickness, and the living room length, you find a total length of 28¾ inches.

Because this wall is completely contained between the two floors (first story and second story) the height is the floor-to-ceiling height of 9½ inches. These dimensions will establish the outline for the wall as shown in Fig. 7–14. Then add the window and door locations for the kitchen from Fig. 6–26, and the archway from the living room wall shown in Fig. 6–32. On the kitchen side, the door is located at 2½ inches on the inside; to this the exterior wall thickness of ⅜ inch must be added to establish the door location of 2⅞ inches. Add the exterior wall thickness to the window location also, for a total dimension of 7⅞ inches. On the living room side locate the arch 9½ inches from the end, because this wall will butt against the inside of the exterior living room wall.

Fig. 7–14   Kitchen/living room wall pattern

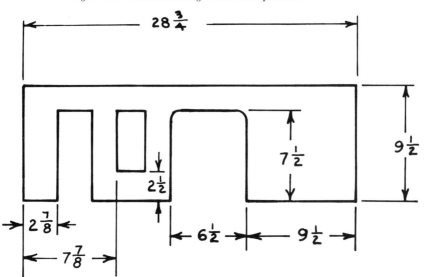

Bedroom/Master Bedroom Wall Pattern

To establish the length of this common wall, refer to the bedroom floor plan (Fig. 6–38) and the master bedroom floor plan (Fig. 6–43). By adding the exterior bedroom wall thickness, the length of bedroom, the interior partition thickness, and the length of master bedroom, you arrive at a total length of 28¾ inches.

To establish the height of this wall, add the bedroom floor-to-ceiling height, and the attic floor thickness, to get a total height of 9⅜ inches.

Part of the wall must be beveled at the top to fit the slope of the bedroom roof. The length of this bevel is determined by the length of the bedroom section. To establish this length, add the length plus two wall thicknesses to get 12¾ inches.

On the master bedroom side the wall height will be limited to the second story floor-to-ceiling height of 9 inches because this wall must fit between the second story floor and the attic floor. The length of this section is equal to the inside dimension of the master bedroom—16 inches.

With these dimensions the outline for the bedroom/master bedroom common wall can be generated as shown in Fig. 7–15. To this outline, the locations of the doors must be added. Refer to the bedroom floor plan

Fig. 7–15 Bedroom/master bedroom wall pattern

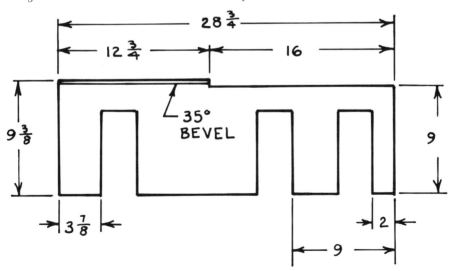

in Fig. 6–38, and note location of the door at 3½ inches; to this add the exterior wall thickness of ⅜ inch to get a 3⅞ inch location for the bedroom door. Then refer to the master bedroom wall in Fig. 6–44, and note locations of doors at 2 inches and 9 inches. (The exterior wall is not included in these dimensions because it already exists.) Add these dimensions and required opening sizes to the outline and complete common wall pattern in Fig. 7–15.

Porch/Living Room Wall Pattern

To establish the width of this wall section refer to the living room floor plan in Fig. 6–30. The total inside width of the living room is 11 inches, *less* the angled portion of 3 inches, for a total of 8 inches. To this 8-inch dimension must be *added* the ⁵⁄₃₂ inch to compensate for the beveled edge, thus making the total width of 8⁵⁄₃₂ inches.

Next, establish the height of the porch/living room exterior wall, by adding first floor thickness, the first story floor-to-ceiling height, the second story floor thickness, the second story floor-to-ceiling height, and the attic floor thickness, to give a height of 19⅝ inches.

Because this height will interfere with the porch floor on the first story and the porch roof on the second story, cutouts are required. Because of the width of the porch, these cutouts will be 7 inches long. These dimensions will generate the outline shown in Fig. 7–16. The door location can be established from the living room floor plan shown in Fig. 6–30. Add the bevel notation and the door opening dimensions to complete the pattern.

Attic Wall Pattern

The dimensions for this piece have already been established by the opposite exterior wall shown in Fig. 7–10. The length will correspond to the established length of 23⅜ inches and the height of the front corner will be 6⅜ inches and the bevel is also common. The height at the back of the house however will be 6 inches (front height of 6⅜ inches *minus* the thickness of the attic floor of ⅜ inch) so that it will not interfere with the lower wall section. The length of the 6⅜-inch section at the front wall be governed by the amount of overhang at the attic floor of 3 inches *less* the allowance for the bevel cut, which is ⁵⁄₃₂ inch, for a total length of 2²⁷⁄₃₂. This dimension can be rounded up to assure a tight fit. With these dimensions the pattern in Fig. 7–17 can be generated.

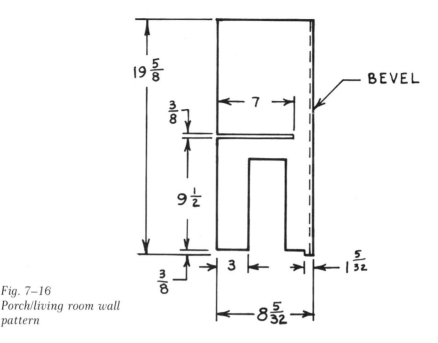

Fig. 7–16
*Porch/living room wall
pattern*

Roof Patterns

The roof for this house is composed of two separate sections. The smaller section is over the bedroom area; the larger section will enclose the entire attic area over the master bedroom, hallway, and bathroom. Each roof section is comprised of two identical parts, which form an inverted V joined together at the roof ridge. Each part will require a bevel to match the adjoining part.

Bedroom Roof

The length of this roof section will join the larger portion of the house at the attic wall, so the gable overhang allowance will only be needed on one end. To establish the length of the bedroom roof section, add the length of bedroom, the exterior wall thickness, and the suggested overhang of ⅝ inch, to get a length of 13 inches.

The width of the bedroom roof gable can be measured on Fig. 7–9, to establish this dimension at approximately 7⅝ inches. The width of the bedroom roof section can then be calculated by adding the gable width, the front wall thickness, and the suggested overhang (1 inch) to get a width of 9 inches. With these dimensions the pattern for the bedroom roof can be established as in Fig. 7–18. Then indicate the bevel at the top to match the roof slope and note that two pieces are required.

Attic Roof

To calculate the length of the attic roof, refer to the end wall shown in Fig. 7–10, and add the length of attic wall, the thickness of front gable, the thickness of rear gable, the overhang at front gable (1 inch), and the overhang at rear gable, to get total length of 26⅛ inches.

Next establish width of attic roof section, by measuring the length along roofline in Fig. 7–11, which gives approximately 10 inches (including wall thickness). To this measurement, add amount of overhang desired of 1 inch, thus making the total width of the attic roof 11 inches. These dimensions will generate the pattern shown in Fig. 7–19. Indicate the required bevel on top edge, for flush fit with adjoining roof section.

Interior Partitions

The first partition is the common partition between kitchen and stairwell. Refer to the kitchen wall elevation drawing in Fig. 6–25 for dimensions and location of arch. To Fig. 6–25 add the first story floor-to-ceiling dimension of 9½ inches and length of 12 inches, to establish the partition as shown in Fig. 7–20.

The stairwell partition is located adjacent to the kitchen wall. The dimensions for this can be obtained from the dining room floor plan in Fig. 6–29. It will appear as 3 inches wide and 9½ inches high (floor to ceiling height) as shown in Fig. 7–21.

The next wall to consider is the staircase wall. Because of the many options possible with this wall, the selection is left to the discretion of the builder. The staircase can be (1) completely enclosed, requiring a wall from floor to ceiling; (2) open staircase with paneling; (3) open staircase with built-in desk or bookshelves, or (4) open wrought-iron staircase.

The first partition to consider on the second story is the bedroom/hallway partition. Refer to the bedroom floor plan in Fig. 6–22 and the bedroom wall drawing in Fig. 6–24 to obtain the necessary dimensions. The height of the wall is the floor-to-ceiling height of 9 inches as shown in Fig. 6–40. The length of the wall is the length of the bedroom as shown in Fig. 6–38, or 12 inches, with the door located at ½ inch from the back side. These dimensions will generate the pattern shown in Fig. 7–22.

The next partition to be considered is the closet/bathroom partition; it will be installed before the hallway partition. Refer to the floor plan shown

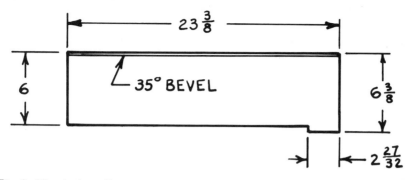

Fig. 7–17   Attic wall pattern

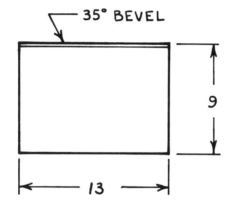

Fig. 7–18   Bedroom roof pattern

Fig. 7–19   Attic roof pattern

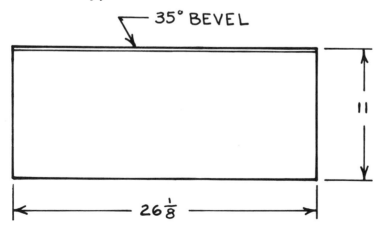

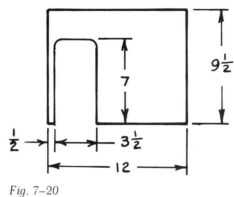

Fig. 7–20
Kitchen/stairwell partition pattern

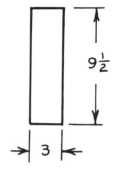

Fig. 7–21
Stairwell partition pattern

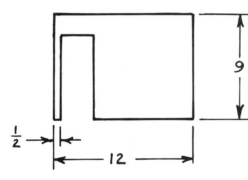

Fig. 7–22
Bedroom/hallway partition pattern

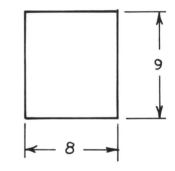

Fig. 7–23
Closet/bathroom partition pattern

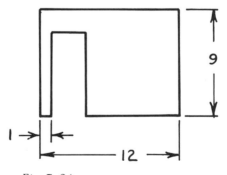

Fig. 7–24
Bathroom/hallway partition pattern

in Fig. 6–41 and note length of closet to be 8 inches. The height of the wall will be the same as the floor-to-ceiling height, or 9 inches. These dimensions will produce the pattern for the closet wall shown in Fig. 7–23.

The next partition to be defined is the bathroom and hallway. Refer to the floor plan in Fig. 6–41 and note length of hallway to be 12 inches. Height of wall will be the floor-to-ceiling height of 9 inches, with bathroom door located 1 inch from the back edge of the house. These dimensions will generate the pattern shown in 7–24.

Sun Porch Patterns

The sun porch was left until now because it is treated as a separate assembly. It can be included with the house or eliminated at the preference of the builder. In establishing the necessary patterns, refer to the sun porch floor plan in Fig. 6–36 and the wall sections shown in Fig. 6–37 for dimensions. The inside width of the center window section in Fig. 6–37 is 3½ inches; to establish the outside measurement, add the required 5/32 inch to each side to compensate for the bevel. Thus the total width will be 3 13/16 inches. The inside floor-to-ceiling height is 7⅝ inches. To determine the overall outside height, add the ceiling thickness of ⅜ inch to the 7⅝-inch floor-to-ceiling dimension to get a total of 8 inches. Then generate the drawing for the wall section as shown in Fig. 7–25. Indicate bevel required to match adjoining wall section, and the dimensions of window opening.

In establishing the dimensions for the side walls of the sun porch, refer to the floor plan in Fig. 6–36 and note width of side panel at 2 inches. To this add the 5/32 inch required for the bevel cut, and establish total width at 2 5/32. Height of panel will be the same as for the window sections at 8 inches. Pattern for the side walls is shown in Fig. 7–26.

Refer to the sun porch floor plan shown in Fig. 6–36 to establish the dimensions for the ceiling. Overall length will be noted at 8½ inches, side wall width of 2 inches; and overall width of 4½ inches. The corners will be angled at 45° for 2½ inches each way. These dimensions will generate the pattern for the sun porch roof shown in Fig. 7–27.

The dimensions for the sun porch roof crown shown in Fig. 7–28 were generated to make it from a single piece of pine and not plywood as the rest of the components are. It could also be fabricated in segmented pieces. A ¼-inch bead was routed on the bottom side to produce the desired effect; this can be altered to fit individual taste. The detail of the railing on the sun porch is shown in Fig. 6–30, so no additional drawings are required.

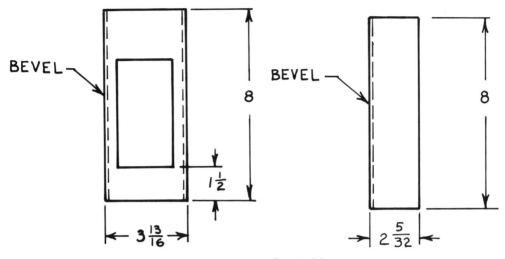

Fig. 7–25
Sun porch window pattern
(three panels required)

Fig. 7–26
Sun porch side wall pattern
(two sections required)

Foundation Wall

This area of miniature construction has many solutions, all of which have merit. Some houses lend themselves well to no foundation at all; others with a high foundation wall can provide drawer space for storing additional material. Some have a foundation height requiring only one step, while still others have been built with full-sized basements and completely finished with laundry room and den.

With the extreme amount of variations possible, the final decision rests with the builder. The only requirement when a foundation is included is to make it high enough to accomodate evenly spaced steps, whether it be only a single step or a dozen.

To establish the foundation height refer to the front and side views of the porch shown in Figs. 6–47 and 6–48. When the thickness of the porch floor of ⅜ inch is included the total rise of the steps is 2½ inches. Thus the foundation height in this particular miniature house is 2⅛ inches. This permits four step risers equally spaced at ⅝-inch scale (8 inches actual).

When establishing the location of the foundation with respect to the walls, allow the foundation wall to extend ³⁄₁₆ inch beyond the inside dimensions of the house, or one-half the total wall thickness. This is done

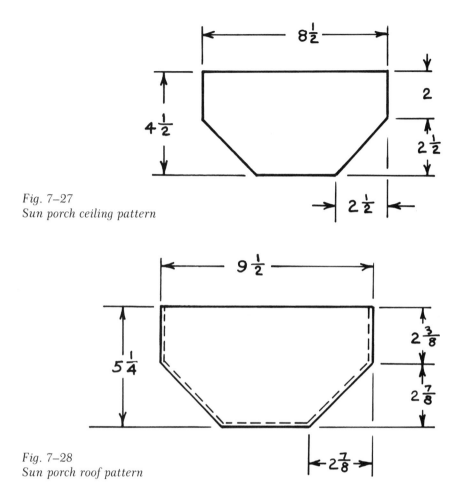

Fig. 7–27
Sun porch ceiling pattern

Fig. 7–28
Sun porch roof pattern

for several reasons: (1) the protrusion will support any hinged wall; (2) it permits use of thinner material for foundation wall (and thus lighter in weight); and (3) it accentuates the break between wall and foundation (which in my opinion improves appearance). When installing a foundation under a *porch* area, recess it approximately ⅜ inch, to permit installing lattice work under the porch if desired. The pattern and dimensions used for this foundation are shown in Fig. 7–29.

The two center crossbraces shown are not necessary, although they add additional support to the floor and strengthen the foundation wall. In normal circumstances each individual piece would be identified by a pattern layout. But because these parts all have the same common thick-

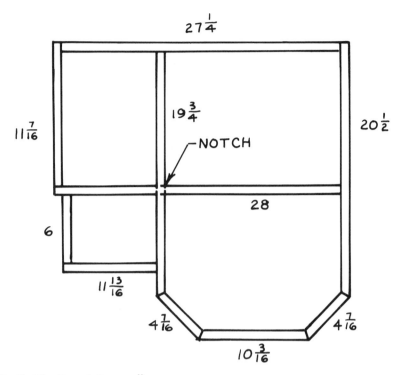

Fig. 7–29   Foundation wall

ness of ¾ inch, and the same common height of 2⅛ inches the only variable is the length. These lengths were determined by the method used to define the complete assembly. Therefore if a different method is employed to develop the foundation assembly, then most if not all, the dimensions would change. For those reasons it seemed prudent not to generate the individual drawings.

Porch Detail Patterns

The porch pillars and the spindles will not be detailed because they are common items that can be purchased and therefore are a standard dimension. To establish the dimensions for trim at the porch ceiling, refer to the elevation views of the porch in Fig. 6–47 and note the height of the panel is 1 inch and length is 5⅝ inches for the larger section. Observing the bracket detail in Fig. 6–49 it can be noted to be 1 inch long. Use a piece of graph paper and lay out the dimensions already established.

Then locate the center of the panel to generate the outline of the part as shown in Fig. 7–30. Because the dimensions on the porch side panel are the same, an additional sketch will not be required for that. It can be noted that the other front panel is the same height but somewhat shorter; therefore, the length can be superimposed on the first section as shown by the dotted lines in Fig. 7–30. By eliminating the two outside cuts (¼R) the pattern will be the same.

The width of the porch railing should be the same width as the pillars, or ⅜ inch, with a thickness of 5/32 inch, and cut to the same length as the ceiling panels or 5⅝ inches. Dimensions of the railing are shown in Fig. 7–31. Two railings will be required on the front and two on the side.

The dimensions for the individual steps can be generated from the porch elevation drawing in Figs. 6–47 and 6–48. The width of the tread will be 5 inches and (knowing that a standard step is actually 9 inches deep,) the depth can be established at ¾ inch in scale; for the thickness use ⅛ inch. With these dimensions the pattern for the individual step can be generated as shown in Fig. 7–32.

Next the base for the steps must be considered. Refer to porch elevation drawings in Figs. 6–47 and 6–48 and note width at the bottom to be 2¼ inches and the height to be 2½ inches, which includes the porch floor thickness. To obtain the correct height for the base, the floor thickness of ⅜ inch will have to be subtracted from the overall height for a total of 2⅛ inches high. The height of the step riser is known to be 8 inches (actual) or ⅝ inch scale. The individual step thickness has already been established as ⅛ inch, so the bottom step will be located at ½ inch from the bottom. Each succeeding step will be located at the proper ⅝ inch as shown in the pattern for the step base in Fig. 7–33. The depth of each individual step tread was established at ¾ inch, so to allow for an overhang the step notches will be ⅝ inch deep also. The thickness of each step support should be ¼ inch.

The sketch for the porch brackets in Fig. 6–49 is sufficiently detailed to use as a pattern, therefore no additional drawing will be required.

Chimney Detail Patterns

The sketch for the chimney in Fig. 6–51 needs to be defined as several pieces, therefore several drawings will be required. The base of the chimney could be produced from a single piece of lumber, but there would be a lot of wasted material and energy. Use a ¾-inch pine board that is 3½ inches wide and 33 inches long, then indicate angles of 35 degrees on one end to match slope of roof, as shown in Fig. 7–34. To increase this width to 5½ inches wide at the base, add 1-inch pieces to each side,

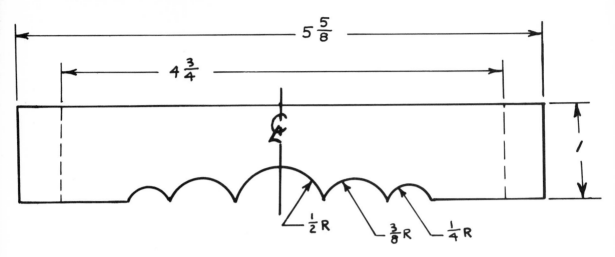

Fig. 7–30   *Porch ceiling trim pattern*

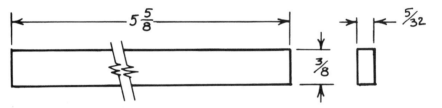

Fig. 7–31   *Porch railing pattern*

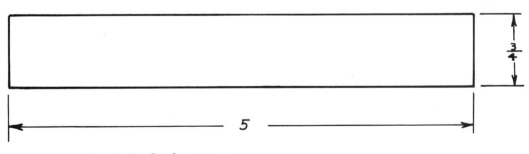

Fig. 7–32   *Porch step pattern*

which are 7½ inches long and then angled at 45 degrees. Then prepare drawing as shown in Fig. 7–35.

The chimney stack at the top can be made from three pieces, the cap and two identical parts for the remaining part of the chimney. Make these parts 4 inches long, and cut out the roof angle of 35° to make an inverted V. This part must be 3½ inches wide to correspond to the base of the chimney, as shown in Fig. 7–36. Make two pieces to give an overall thickness of 1½ inches. The cap is ¾ inch high and it must be wide enough to cover the 3½ inch width of the stack, and must be deep enough to cover the thickness of 1½ inches. By making the cap 4 inches wide and 2 inches deep there will be a ¼-inch overhang all around. Define this part as shown in Fig. 7–37.

Materials List

A materials list is an extremely useful tool in determining the required amount of plywood for the house. The list will not only contain the overall dimensions of the various parts but will also identify the quantity of each part that is required. Include in the list only those components that are fabricated from plywood and include the drawing number for a handy quick reference.

One method of establishing the amount of plywood that will be required would be to determine the square footage of each component and then

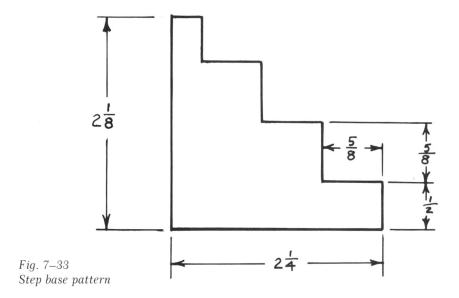

Fig. 7–33
Step base pattern

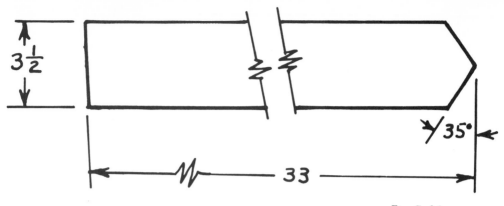

Fig. 7–34
Main chimney piece

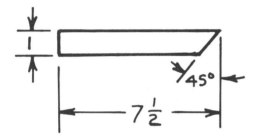

Fig. 7–35
Side chimney pieces

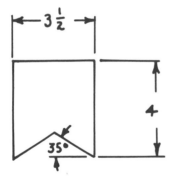

Fig. 7–36
Chimney top piece

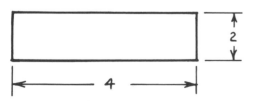

Fig. 7–37
Chimney cap pattern

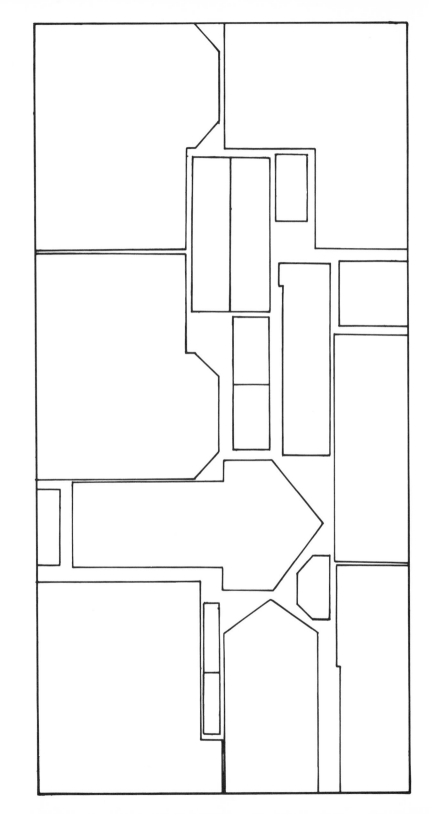

Fig. 7–38
Pattern layout

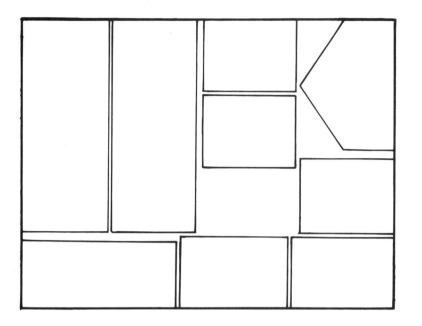

Fig. 7–38
(continued)

obtain the total by the summation of these components. This will generate a close approximation and does not allow for any scrap. To allow for scrap and mixmatch add 10 percent more plywood to the total.

A better, and more exact, method would be to make a scaled drawing, of the *outline* of each part, on graph paper, then cut out the individual parts and fit these pieces to a scaled drawing of a sheet of plywood (4′ × 8′). This will allow for maximum rearranging of the parts, until the best fit on the plywood can be obtained. This approach is a little more tedious but it definitely assures the best utilization of the plywood and the minimum amount of scrap.

The pattern layout shown in Fig. 7–38 requires one 4-foot-by-8-foot sheet of plywood and an additional 3-foot-by-4-foot panel. This pattern is only one solution to solving the pattern arrangement. There are many other satisfactory ways of fitting the pattern to the required amount of plywood. If you devise a more simplified arrangement, by all means use it.

Materials List for Miniature House

ITEM	PART	FIGURE NUMBER	DIMENSIONS (IN INCHES)	QUANTITY
A	First Floor	7-6	23⅜ × 28⅜	1
B	Second Floor	7-7	23⅜ × 28⅜	1
C	Attic Floor	7-8	23⅜ × 28⅜	1
D	Gable, kitchen side	7-9	12 × 23⅞	1
E	Dining room side wall	7-10	23⅝ × 25⅝	1
F	Front Gable	7-11	16¾ × 31¼	1
G	Back Gable	7-12	16¾ × 12	1
H	L.R. corner wall	7-13	4⅝ × 19¼	2
I	kitchen/L.R. wall	7-14	9½ × 28¾	1
J	Bedroom/M.B.R. wall	7-15	9⅜ × 28¾	1
K	Porch/L.R. wall	7-16	8⁵⁄₃₂ × 19⅝	1
L	Attic wall	7-17	6⅜ × 23⅜	1
M	Bedroom roof	7-18	9 × 13	2
N	Attic roof	7-19	11 × 26⅛	2
O	Kitchen partition	7-20	9½ × 12	1
P	Staircase wall	7-21	3 × 9½	1
Q	Bedroom partition	7-22	9 × 12	1
R	Closet wall	7-23	8 × 9	1
S	Hallway/bath wall	7-24	9 × 12	1
T	Sun porch, window wall	7-25	3¹³⁄₁₆ × 8	3
U	Sun porch, Side wall	7-26	2⁵⁄₃₂ × 8	2
V	Sun porch ceiling	7-27	4½ × 8½	1

8
CONSTRUCTION AND ASSEMBLY

Before starting the construction of the miniature house, refer to Figs. 8–1 and 8–2, which show the front and back views of the miniature house. The view of the open back has the interior partitions removed to make the assembly process slightly more comprehensible. The construction of the individual parts and the assembly of the house will be done simultaneously, to assure proper fit and avoid unnecessary pitfalls. The dimensions for this particular house were established to give a snug fit all around and in some cases (where a bevel is required) the dimensions have been rounded upwards to obtain a tight fit, so a slight trim might be required in these areas.

In all instances, the individual parts should be checked for proper fit, and any necessary adjustments made, prior to installing permanently to house structure with glue and nails. After proper fit has been established on each of the parts, fill any voids in the plywood edges with wood putty to eliminate any weak spots in the plywood, before gluing and nailing the piece in place.

When constructing the individual parts, refer to the materials list, the overall pattern layout in Fig. 7–38 and the individual part pattern as it is identified by the respective figure number.

Floor Assembly

1. Cut the pattern for the first floor, A, to the dimensions shown in Fig. 7–6. Sand edges lightly to remove any splinters.

2. Cut the pattern for the second floor, B, to the dimensions shown in Fig. 7–7. Check size and squareness with pattern of the first floor, A,

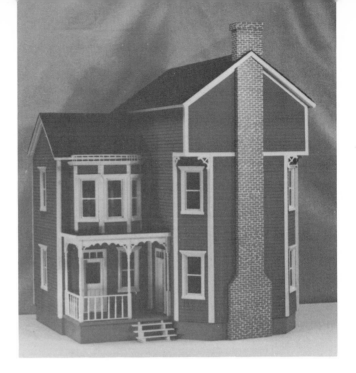

Fig. 8–1
Dollhouse (front view)

Fig. 8–2
Dollhouse (back view)

before locating staircase opening. To cut the staircase opening, first drill ⅜-inch starter holes for the sabre sawblade clearance, then cut the opening to the dimensions indicated. Sand sawcut edges lightly to remove any splinters.

3. Cut the pattern for the attic floor, C, to the dimensions shown in Fig. 7–8. Check size and squareness with the pattern of the first floor, A, and the pattern of the second floor, B, then sand sawcut edges lightly.

Kitchen Gable Assembly

4. Cut the pattern for the kitchen side gable, D, to the dimensions shown in Fig. 7–9. Check squareness and fit of the gable with the edge of the first floor, A, before locating window openings. To cut window openings, drill ⅜-inch starter holes for the sabre sawblade, then cut to the dimensions indicated. Sand sawcut edges lightly to remove any edge splinters.

Dining Room Wall Assembly

5. Cut the pattern for the dining room side wall, E, to the dimensions shown in Fig. 7–10. Check squareness with the edge of the first floor, A, using a framing square, before locating the required window openings. To cut the window openings, first drill ⅜-inch starter holes for the sabre sawblade, then cut window openings to selected dimensions.

If this wall is to be hinged, first cut out the portion indicated by the dotted line, then bevel the forward edge, as indicated, at the required angle. At this point, the assembly will be started, refer to Fig. 8–3, for view of the assembled walls and floors. Attach the kitchen gable, D, in the proper position to the first floor, A, flush with the back edge, with glue and nails. Then attach the dining room side wall, E, to the opposite end of the first floor, A, flush to the back edge, with glue and nails, removing any excess glue. Next, install the second floor, B, between the kitchen gable, D, and the dining room end wall, E, at the required 9½ inch, floor-to-ceiling height, on both ends, with glue and nails. Make this dimension as accurate as possible, along both ends of the walls. Apply glue clamps to assure a tight fit between walls and floors, and also to assure that the assembly will remain square. Remove any excess glue.

At this particular point in the construction of the miniature house, it may be desirable to do the decorating of the interior walls of the kitchen, dining room, bedroom, bathroom, and closet. The extreme accessibility that is provided by the walls being open on both sides presents an ideal

Fig. 8–3   Floor assembly

situation for applying wallpaper or paint. The openness permits easy alignment and adjusting the wallpaper pattern from either end, thus assuring squareness of the pattern with walls and ceiling.

Kitchen/Living Room Wall Assembly

6. Cut the pattern for the kitchen/living room wall, I, to the dimensions shown in Fig. 7–14, then check wall for fit as shown in Fig. 8–4. Locate openings for doors and window. To cut the openings, drill ⅜-inch starter holes for the sabre sawblade, then cut to size. Sand sawcut edges, and install the wall with glue and nails as shown in Fig. 8–5, flush with the dining room side wall, E and flush with the front of the kitchen gable, D. Remove any excess glue.

Prior to the permanent installation of this wall section, it may be desirable to complete the interior decorating of this piece, with either paint or wallpaper. The completely exposed wall section permits accessibility for easy application and alignment of wallpaper, wainscoting, or painting. If wallpaper is used, be sure to align the pattern, square with the floor

Fig. 8–4   *Checking for proper fit*

Fig. 8–5   *Installing kitchen/living room wall*

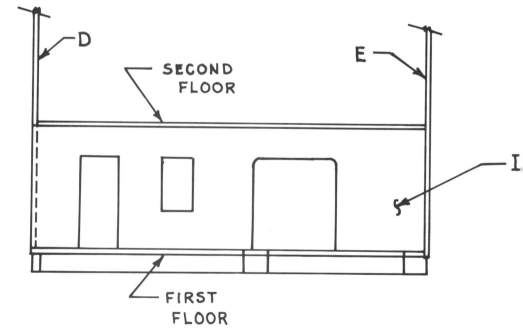

and ceiling, so that it will match the pattern of the adjoining wall at the corner.

Bedroom/Master Bedroom Wall Assembly

7. Cut the pattern for the bedroom/master bedroom common wall, J, to dimensions indicated in Fig. 7–15. Check for proper fit between the second story floor and attic floor as shown in Fig. 8–6, then locate door openings. To cut door openings, first drill ⅜-inch starter holes for the sabre sawblade, then cut to the required size. Sand sawcut edges lightly. Remember to bevel the top edge of this wall on the bedroom side only, then sand edges lightly. Check for proper fit before installing permanently, with glue and nails. On the bedroom side, this section should overlap the bedroom exterior wall and the bevel on the top side should match the roof pitch angle. If necessary, make required adjustments to bevel. Then install flush with the front edge of the kitchen gable, D, and flush to the inside of the dining room side wall, E. Attach with glue and nails. Remove any excess glue. (Prior to permanent installation of this

Fig. 8–6   Checking for proper fit

section, it may be desirable to complete the interior decorating first, then install the completed wall section.)

Porch/Living Room Wall Assembly

8. Cut the pattern for the porch/living room wall, K, to the dimensions indicated in Fig. 7–16. Cut the groove width to match the second floor, B, and also notch panel to fit with the first floor, A. Check for proper fit, then bevel front edge and locate door opening. Sand sawcut edges lightly, then install as shown in Fig. 8–7, flush against the bedroom wall, J, and the exterior kitchen wall, I, with glue and nails, removing any excess glue.

Attic Wall Assembly

9. Cut the pattern for the attic wall, L, to dimensions indicated in Fig. 7–17. Adjust panel so it will fit flush with the front of the attic floor, C, if necessary. Bevel the top edge, and sand lightly, then install as shown in Fig. 8–8 with glue and nails. Remove excess glue.

Gable Wall Assemblies

10. Cut the pattern for the front gable, F, to dimensions indicated in Fig. 7–11. Bevel both front edges of the lower section. Then check for proper fit at the living room floor, A, and at the bevel of the attic wall, L, and also flush with the outside wall. Sand sawcut edges lightly, then glue and nail in place, to the dining room side wall, E, and at the proper height to the first and second floors, A and B, as shown in Fig. 8–9. Remove excess glue. This is another section where it may be desirable to complete the wall decorating before permanently installing in place, because of the lack of accessibility once it is installed.

11. Cut the pattern for the back gable, G, to the dimensions shown in Fig. 7–12. (If access to the attic is desired, then cut out the dotted line pattern.) Install this back gable on the back end of attic floor, C, and also attach it to the attic side wall, L, and the dining room side wall, E, with glue and nails. Remove any excess glue.

Corner Wall Assembly

12. Cut the patterns for two living room corner walls, H, to the dimensions indicated in Fig. 7–13. Bevel both sides of both pieces, and check for fit. A slight adjustment of $1/32$ inch may be necessary. When

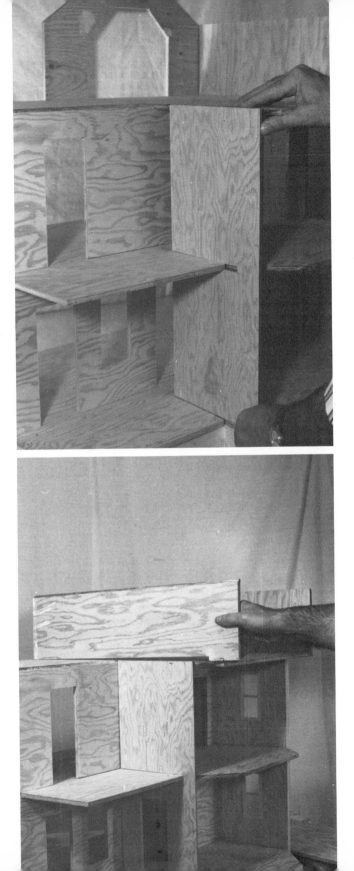

Fig. 8–7
Porch/living room wall
assembly

Fig. 8–8
Attic wall assembly

proper fit has been attained, locate window openings with a framing square on the center of the wall section. Cut out the window openings to the required dimensions with a sabre saw. Sand sawcut edges; then install both wall sections as shown in Fig. 8–10, one on each side of the front gable, F, with glue and nails. Remove any excess glue.

Roof Assemblies

13. Cut the patterns for two bedroom roof sections, M, to the dimensions indicated in Fig. 7–18. Bevel edges at the roof ridge to match each other. Before assembling, it may be desirable to cut a roof support to fit the inside of the bedroom roof at the attic wall side as shown in Fig. 8–11. Cut the support from any piece of scrap wood, to the same pattern and angle as the kitchen gable, D, then glue in place on the attic wall. Adding this support is not an absolute necessity, but it does help with the alignment of the roof sections and adds additional support to the bedroom roof. Maintain a snug fit of the roof panels at the roof ridge while assembling them to the kitchen gable, D, and the attic wall, L. Attach roof panels with glue and nails; remove excess glue.

14. Cut to fit patterns for two attic roof sections, N, to dimensions shown in Fig. 7–19. Bevel the edges to match each other at the roof ridge, then sand sawcut edges lightly. Attach roof sections to the front gable, F, and back gable, G, as shown in Fig. 8–12, with glue and nails, while maintaining a snug fit at the roof ridge. Then remove excess glue.

If the outer roof section is to be *hinged* then proceed as follows: Cut outer panel ⅛ inch wider (or 11⅛ inches), bevel and then cut a 3-inch strip from the beveled side. Attach this 3-inch roof section, along with the other complete roof section, to the front and back gable ends, with glue and nails, while maintaining a snug fit at the roof ridge. Then remove any excess glue. The remaining roof section will be attached to the 3-inch section with butt hinges and screws, but *do not* attach to gable ends with glue or nails.

Interior Partition Assemblies

Interior partitions should only be dry fit to assure proper fit. Leaving these partitions loose, at this time, will facilitate the interior decorating. Once the interior of the house has been decorated, these partitions can be permanently attached to their respective positions by gluing in place.

15. Cut the pattern for the kitchen/stairwell wall, O, to the dimensions shown in Fig. 7–20 and check for alignment with stairwell opening and the living room wall. It should fit to the edge of the arch. Use a combination square or tri-square to assure wall is perpendicular to the floor

Fig. 8–9
Front gable assembly

Fig. 8–10
Corner wall assembly

Fig. 8–11
Roof support piece

Fig. 8–12
Attic roof assembly

and ceiling as shown in Fig. 8–13. Then locate door opening and cut out. Sand sawcut edges lightly to remove any splinters.

16. The next wall, in order of assembly, is the wall under the staircase and adjacent to the kitchen wall. Cut the pattern for this staircase wall, P, to the dimensions shown in Fig. 7–21. After sanding lightly, this wall can be attached to the kitchen wall, O, to insure squareness and fit, but do not attach to floor or ceiling at this time.

At this point in the construction, consideration will be given to the staircase. The decision will eventually have to be made regarding an open or an enclosed staircase. And when this decision is made then it must also be determined whether the staircase will be purchased as a ready-made unit or if it will be a custom-made one. The ready-made staircases are discussed in the components section. For detail on construction of a custom-made staircase refer to Chapter 4. If the decision has been reached to utilize a ready-made unit and install it later, then proceed with the remaining construction of the doll house. If on the other hand the decision has been made to install a custom-made staircase, then it would be advisable to construct it at this point. Allow the staircase to be a removable unit so the interior decorating can be completed before permanently installing the staircase.

17. The next interior partition to be considered is the bedroom staircase wall, Q, on the second level. Cut the pattern as shown in Fig. 7–22, and only dry fit to the structure. This wall should match the stairwell cutout and the master bedroom wall, J, as shown in Fig. 8–14. Here again check perpendicularity with a combination square as shown in Fig. 8–15, and adjust wall if necessary. Then locate and cut out door opening and sand lightly.

18. Cut the pattern for the closet wall, R, to the dimensions shown in Fig. 7–23. Then dry fit between ceiling and floor while checking for fit with the dining room side wall, E. Do not install in place until the wall is decorated with either paint or wallpaper.

19. Cut the pattern for the hallway/bath wall, S, to the dimensions shown in Fig. 7–24. Make the door opening, then check for fit with closet wall, R, and master bedroom wall, J. Assure perpendicularity with a combination square but do not attach to floor or ceiling until decorating is complete.

Sun Porch Assembly

20. Cut the pattern for the sun porch ceiling, V, to the dimensions shown in Fig. 7–27. Make sure the corners are cut at 45° to obtain three equally dimensioned sections for mating the three window panels, then sand lightly to remove any edge splinters.

Fig. 8–13
Kitchen wall assembly

Fig. 8–14
Bedroom wall assembly

Fig. 8–15
Adjusting for perpendicular

21. Next, cut three sun porch window walls, to the dimensions shown in Fig. 7–25. Cut window openings to required dimensions and bevel both sides of all three pieces, and sand lightly. Then check for proper fit with the sun porch ceiling, V. If corners are mismatched, adjust as required, then attach window walls to the sun porch ceiling with glue and nails, removing any excess glue. (Note: window is located closer to the floor than to the ceiling in these panels only.)

22. Next, cut the two sun porch side walls, U, to the dimensions shown in Fig. 7–26. Bevel one edge of each panel, then check for fit with porch ceiling and window panels. Sand lightly before attaching to sun porch ceiling, V, with glue and nails. The total assembly should appear as in Fig. 8–16.

The remaining items necessary to complete the sun porch are the roof cap and the railing. Proceed by cutting the sun porch roof cap to the pattern and dimensions shown in Fig. 7–28. Assure that the corners are cut at 45 degrees, then proceed to cut the edge of the roof cap with a bead shaped router bit to obtain the desired configuration.

To locate the pattern for the railing on top of the roof cap refer to Fig. 8–17. Measure ⅜ inch from the front edge of the roof cap as shown. This will establish the location of the dowels. Then start at the center of each of the three window sections and measure ¾ inch spacings for the dowels to obtain five dowels per section. For each of the two side railings, space two dowels ¾ inch apart also. Then drill ⅛-inch diameter holes approximately ⅛ inch deep at all the dowel locations.

For the railing, use ⅜ inch wide by ³⁄₁₆ inch thick strips of basswood or pine. Then, starting with the center section, drill five ⅛-inch holes to fit the pattern established for the roof cap. Then proceed with the remaining sections, on separate pieces of railings, and establish the matching hole pattern for each one. Then cut nineteen dowels, ¾ inch long, from ⅛-inch diameter stock. Assemble dowels in the roof cap section and place the railing on top of the dowels. At the intersection of the two rails cut the angle to fit. Because of the possible variations in this assembly it is best to cut the lengths of railings at the time of assembly. If a slight mismatch occurs between the corners of the railing, fill this gap with wood putty and sand smooth. Then attach this completed roof cap section to the top of the sun porch assembly, and fit this total assembly to the house against the exterior bedroom wall (Fig. 8–18).

Foundation Wall Assembly

The foundation wall could have been assembled and attached to the first floor, A, at the beginning of the house construction. However, it was left

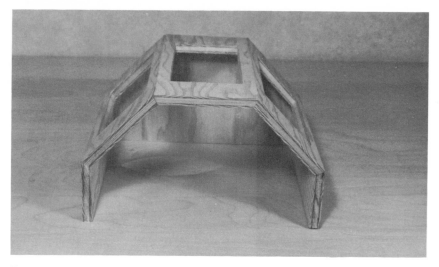

Fig. 8–16   Sun porch assembly

Fig. 8–17   Sun porch roof cap

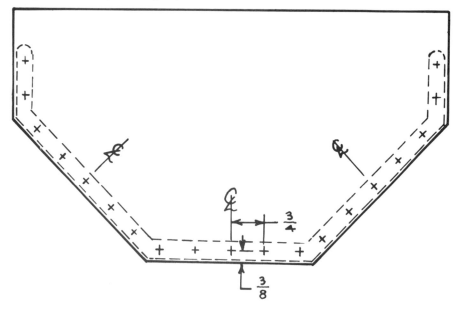

Fig. 8–18   Sun porch attached to house

until now to assure squareness with house and proper alignment with the side walls. (This is also an opportunity to increase the height of the foundation if that is desired. Just remember to increase it in ⅝ inch increments for each additional step riser that will be required.)

The assembly features and the dimensions of the individual parts are shown as the top view in Fig. 7–29. There are many alternatives to the physical layout of the foundation wall. The view of the foundation wall assembled to the miniature house is shown in Fig. 8–19. Each piece is made from ¾-inch thick stock that is 2⅛ inches wide. Cut the required number of pieces to the required dimensions. The parts that require a bevel are indicated on the assembly drawing. The two parts that intersect in the middle will have to be notched to accept the mating part for a proper fit. Then assemble parts as indicated and attach to the bottom of the house with nails and glue. Position foundation assembly flush with the open back side of the house. Nails used in the foundation wall should be countersunk and the holes filled with wood putty to obtain a smooth appearance to the foundation wall. Then sand edges and corners of the foundation wall as required.

Porch Assembly

The porch assembly was included at this point to allow for finishing the house at this state of completion by either painting the exterior or applying stucco rather than applying siding. If siding is to be applied, then the best procedure is to install the porch on a temporary basis, to allow for removal before applying siding and painting. When the porch is finally installed on a permanent basis, the exterior kitchen wall and living room wall should first have the siding installed in place and painted. The porch assembly is shown in Fig. 8–20.

Materials List for Porch Assembly

ITEM	PART	FIGURE NUMBER	DIMENSIONS (IN INCHES)	QUANTITY
A	Trim	7-30	$\frac{1}{4} \times 1 \times 4\frac{3}{4}$	1
B	Trim	7-30	$\frac{1}{4} \times 1 \times 5\frac{5}{8}$	2
C	Railing	7-31	$\frac{5}{32} \times \frac{3}{8} \times 5\frac{5}{8}$	4
D	Bracket	6-33	$\frac{1}{8} \times 1 \times 1$	6
E	Porch posts purchased		$\frac{3}{8} \times \frac{3}{8} \times 12$	4
F	Porch Spindles purchased		$\frac{1}{4} \times 2\frac{1}{4} \times 2\frac{1}{8}$	3
G	Step Supports	7-33	$\frac{1}{4} \times 2\frac{1}{4} \times 2\frac{1}{8}$	2
H	Steps	7-32	$\frac{1}{8} \times \frac{3}{4} \times 5$	3

1. Cut the pattern for the trim, A, to the required dimensions in Fig. 7–30, with a jigsaw. This is the smaller part, so cut to the dotted lines indicated in the pattern and eliminate the $\frac{1}{4}$-inch radius cuts. Sand edges smooth with a fine grade of sand paper.

2. Cut the pattern for two parts for trim B to the outline and dimensions shown in Fig. 7–30 with a jigsaw. This trim will be the full-sized pattern. Sand edges smooth with a fine grade of sand paper. To sand the contours wrap a piece of sandpaper around a $\frac{1}{4}$-inch dowel.

3. Cut the pattern for four railings, C, to dimensions indicated in the material list and in Fig. 7–31. Sand edges lightly.

4. Cut the pattern for six brackets, D, to the dimensions indicated in Fig. 6–33, with a jigsaw. (Tape several together and cut all at one time.) Then sand lightly.

Fig. 8–19   Foundation wall assembly

Fig. 8–20   Porch assembly

5. Cut the four (purchased) porch posts, E, to length to fit the porch floor to ceiling height.

6. Cut the pattern for two step supports, G, to the dimensions required in Fig. 7–33, with a jigsaw. Then sand edges lightly.

7. Cut the pattern for three steps, H, to the dimensions indicated in Fig. 7–32. Sand edges lightly.

8. Lay three porch posts, E, on a flat surface, and place one short trim, A, between the two on the right side, and one longer trim, B, between the two on the left, then glue in place. Remove excess glue. Apply a weight until glue dries.

9. Between two railings, C, install six porch spindles, F, equally spaced. When proper spacing is obtained, glue in place. Apply a weight or clamp until glue dries. Make two of these assemblies. When the glue has dried install one of these assemblies between the two porch posts, E, on the left of previous assembly and flush with the bottom of the porch posts, with glue. Then place this assembly on the front side of the porch.

10. Install remaining railing assembly and remaining porch post, E, on the side of the porch. Add the remaining trim, B, and the six brackets, D, to proper position with glue. Assure that the assembly is square with the porch. Remove excess glue. Do not glue porch posts, E, to the porch to allow for ease of removal.

11. Assemble the three steps, H, to the two step supports, G, with glue and spaced with a 1-inch overhang on each side of the support. This assembly can be attached with glue to the porch foundation and centered between the porch posts.

Chimney Assembly

To construct the components for the chimney, refer to the photograph of the miniature house in Fig. 8–1. All material for the chimney parts will be made from standard ¾-inch pine.

Cut the pattern for the main part of the chimney to the dimensions shown in Fig. 7–34, then check fit with roof line of house, and make any necessary adjustments. The opposite end should be flush with the bottom of the foundation wall. Next, cut the two side pieces of the chimney according to the pattern and the dimensions in Fig. 7–35, then attach one to each side of the main chimney part with glue and nails. Remove excess glue and sand if necessary. Attach complete assembly to the center of the front gable with glue and nails. The gap that will exist at the bottom of the chimney between the foundation and chimney can be fitted with a scrap piece of wood or filled with wood putty. (Because of the variation in foundation construction the amount of this gap will vary with each individual house.)

To construct the chimney stack on top of the roof, refer to Fig. 7–36 and cut two identical parts to the pattern and dimensions shown. Again utilize the standard ¾-inch lumber. Cut the required angle on each part and check the fit with the slope of the roof, adjusting if necessary. Then glue the two pieces together and apply a weight or glue clamp.

Next, refer to Fig. 7–27 and cut the chimney cap to a pattern and the dimensions shown, then attach to the top of the two-piece chimney stack just completed with glue and nails, centered in both directions. Place this assembly on top of the roof and align with the lower section of the chimney, then glue in place, removing any excess glue.

Once the components for the chimney have been cut out and assembled to the house, the builder must decide how the chimney will be finished. It can be finished with the miniature shaped red bricks that are available in sheet form or with individual bricks installed with glue and with or without mortar between the individual bricks. Individual wood bricks can be glued in place and then painted any desired color. The chimney can also be completed with wood sheets of silk-screened red brick. Use the pattern that is crosswise on the sheet. The edges of the sheets can then be beveled to fit the brick pattern around the corners of the chimney, and give it a realistic appearance.

The chimney could also be finished with paper bricks that are available in several sized sheets, of printed brick, from 8½ inches by 11 inches up to the larger sheets of 17 inches by 23 inches. These sheets of printed bricks can be obtained in dark red, light red and tan color. Cut the brick sheets to fit the chimney; after a proper fit has been attained, attach with glue. Press paper firmly to remove any air bubbles, while maintaining the rows of bricks parallel with the foundation. The chimney can be finished as a fieldstone fireplace chimney by applying a ¹⁄₁₆ inch thick coat of plaster of paris and then embedding small pieces of screened gravel into the wet plaster. Another method of finishing the chimney would be to paint it any desired color to either blend with the house color or have it contrast with the basic color.

Window Bracket Assembly

Cut the four master bedroom window brackets as shown in Fig. 6–36 from ⅛-inch lumber. Tape two pieces together before cutting with a jigsaw to acquire a better duplication of the pattern. If siding is to be used, these brackets should be set aside until the corner caps have been glued in place and the siding has been applied.

Corner Trim

Before installing the siding, apply all corner caps, or corner trim, and gable trim to the miniature house. The corner trim on the angled portions of the house will have to be beveled to match the wall angle; make sure that a proper fit is obtained before attaching to house.

The thickness of the corner trim will be dependent on the thickness of the siding used. If the siding thickness is $\frac{1}{16}$ inch, then a $\frac{1}{8}$ inch thick material for corner trim would be an appropriate size. The thinner, $\frac{3}{32}$ thick corner cap material doesn't generate a sufficient depth contrast between siding and corner trim, although it could be used. It's a matter of personal preference.

The width of the corner trim and gable trim, too, is dependent on the thickness of the corner trim. Cut one side of the corner trim to a $\frac{3}{8}$ inch width, then, the adjoining trim will be $\frac{3}{8}$ inch wide plus the thickness of the lumber used. For $\frac{3}{32}$ inch thick trim material, one piece of trim would be $\frac{3}{8}$ inch and the adjoining piece would be $\frac{15}{32}$ inch ($\frac{3}{8}$ plus $\frac{3}{32}$ = $\frac{15}{32}$), because they overlap, thus making the same dimension both ways. For the $\frac{1}{8}$ inch thick material, one side would be $\frac{3}{8}$-inch, the adjoining side would be $\frac{1}{2}$ inch wide, ($\frac{3}{8}$ inch + $\frac{1}{8}$ inch thickness = $\frac{1}{2}$ inch). The trim used for the gable trim should be the thinner of the two corner trim widths, and should be applied flush with the underside of the roof.

When installing the trim utilize a spring clamp as shown in Fig. 8–21 to hold the trim in place while installing. Install the corner caps first as shown in Fig. 8–22, before adding the gable trim. Dry fit individual pieces before attaching in position with glue and nails or staples. On angled walls use the narrow width of trim and bevel to fit. When all the trim has been applied to the house, apply a coat of paint of the desired color. It is much easier to paint now than after the siding is applied. Several coats of paint may be required on the wood trim depending on material used for trim and type of paint utilized.

Siding

Before applying the siding, paint the foundation, porch floor and porch roof to the desired colors. This will eliminate some of the difficulty of painting in the corners and recesses with siding in place. After obtaining the required amount of clapboard siding, cut the siding to cover only a small area at one time. Make the necessary door and window cutouts in this amount of siding. Paint this cut siding to the desired color then place on a flat surface and apply weights to maintain the siding in a flat position

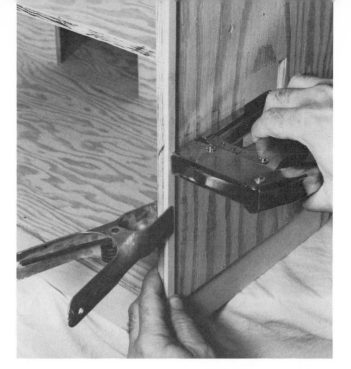

Fig. 8–21
Using spring clamps

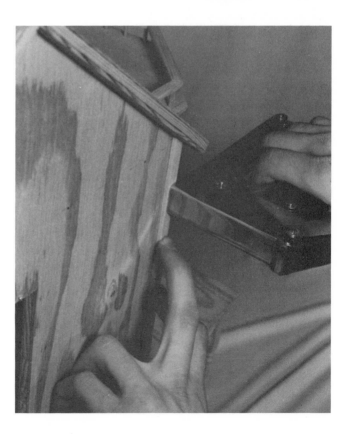

Fig. 8–22
Attaching corner trim

until the paint dries. This material is so thin ($\frac{1}{16}$ inch thick) that when paint is applied it tends to curl up. By placing the required weight on it will prevent the wood from curling.

When the paint on the siding has dried, apply one piece at a time to the house with glue or staples or both. When glue is used, the siding will begin to curl up as with the paint. So here again apply sufficient weight, or clamps, to maintain the section in a completely flat position until the glue has dried. While waiting for the glue to dry, measure and cut siding for another area of the house. Then paint these sections and apply the necessary weight to maintain a flat position on the painted pieces of siding as was done before. By this time the glue on the first piece of siding should be dry enough to attach a second piece. Then proceed as before, applying glue and weights to the second piece of siding.

Siding can be glued and installed in more than one area at a time if the proper amount of weights or clamps can be applied to maintain the siding perfectly flat while glue is drying. Always start applying the siding from the foundation up and always from the same position at the foundation. This will assure that the individual courses of siding (the lap) will always be at the same height on all sides of the house. The second reason, and equally important, for applying the siding from the bottom up is that this siding is undercut at the bottom edge to permit the top section to overlap the bottom portion and assure a tight fit. By coordinating the various operations of cutting, painting and gluing the siding in place, the house can be completed in a short amount of time. Remove the excess glue as soon as possible. Sandpaper attached to a small block of wood can be used to remove excess glue after the glue has dried.

Siding can also be applied with a staple gun only as shown in Fig. 8–23, or with staples and glue. If staples only are used, be prepared to apply a weight to the siding immediately after painting the siding to prevent the natural curling that will be produced by the paint. If glue and staples are used, apply the required weight to the siding to offset the curling effect caused by the glue. When using the staple gun, always align the staple gun with the row of siding in the horizontal plane. If applied in the vertical plane it will chip the edge of the siding and adversely affect the appearance. Use of a spring clamp can also be incorporated but never apply it directly to the siding, for the jaws of the clamp will bite into the wood and leave a noticeable mark.

The siding used for this particular house is the standard sized sheet of clapboard siding that measures $3\frac{1}{2}$ inches wide by 24 inches long by $\frac{1}{16}$ inch thick. The individual lap height is $\frac{3}{8}$ inch. This style of siding is readily available at most miniature specialty shops, and at some hobby stores. Refer to the components section for other sizes and types of siding available.

Fig. 8–23
Attaching siding

Fig. 8–24
Shingle alignment

Shingles

Any standard type shingle can be used. Wood shingles are available in cedar and pine, with a square end, diamond-shaped end or the recent octagon butt end, and also in the round-end, fishscale style. Any of these are satisfactory. Also available are cardboard and asphalt-coated shingles in a variety of shapes. Whatever type is used, start at the lower outside corner of the roof and allow the shingle to overlap the eave and side of the roof a sufficient amount to include the thickness of any trim board that will be added later on. Typical alignment and starting position of the shingles are shown in Fig. 8–24.

Align the first row of shingles with either a framing square or combination square. The first shingle in the first row should be a complete shingle. Lay a starter course of shingles across complete roof, then start the second row of shingles with a half shingle, so that the gaps between shingles are staggered, between adjacent rows. Continue this pattern of alternating full shingle then half shingle, at the roof edge, until the complete roof has been shingled. Check alignment periodically with a framing square to assure proper spacing between rows of shingles.

Roof Trim

The edge of the roof, both at the eave location and gable end will require a trim molding to give the house that final finished look. This is not an absolute necessity but it improves the appearance of the house, especially if it is a bead or cove molding trim rather than a plain surface.

Additional roof brackets can be added to the two gable ends of the house to accent the roof pitch and roof line if desired. There are several styles of gable brackets that could be added to the kitchen gable if a more ornate style is desired.

9
MINIATURE HOUSES, DISPLAY CASES AND SPECIALTY SHOPS

A selection of additional miniature buildings of various shapes and sizes are included in this chapter to show the variation in style and room arrangement. Some of the houses are equipped with removable partitions to maximize the possible variations in room arrangements. These removable partitions also allow for easier access to the interior of the house when redoing the interior decor.

House Styles

Many of the miniature replicas being produced today are a preservation of architectural history. Time and urban sprawl have replaced many of the stalwart structures of the past century. Photographs and memories are the only proof that these structures did exist. Today the Victorian-style train depots and the historic covered bridges have been replaced by "progress." The philosophy of some individuals is that if it is progress, then it has to be good. Fortunately not all people ascribe to that theory. Historical groups and societies are fighting desperately to preserve some of the architectural splendor of the past.

One of the most noticeable efforts is in the San Francisco Bay Area, where organized groups are renovating the nineteenth century Victorian row houses. These are the survivors of the devastating 1906 earthquake. At one time there were 48,000 of these intriguing structures gracing the landscape in the San Francisco Area; today, less than a third of these remain intact. Through the dedicated efforts of a host of people, a large number of these homes are being saved from the wrecking ball. Dedicated craftspeople are devoting time and effort to reproducing the ornate elements of the once stately structures: everything from the siding, cement pillars, wooden spindles, to the elaborate moldings that flank the windows and the doorways. The history that surrounds these elegant structures is truly amazing. There are many photo books that show the architectural splendor that these remarkable homes displayed at the turn of the century, the era of disrepair and neglect during the post war years, and their revitalization during the 1970's.

The San Francisco row house shown in Fig. 9–1 has several unique features incorporated into the structure besides the ornate facade. The front portion was designed in two separate sections, both hinged, to allow easy access to the front areas of the house (Fig. 9–2). Because of the narrow width of the windows and doors, these components had to be custom made, along with the window trim and eave brackets. Most of the trim utilized on this Victorian was built from scratch because the desired sizes were not commercially available.

The brackets flanking the corner windows and also shown on the front gable trim were, for the original house, produced with a fret saw. Today, for the miniature replica, this detail can be produced with a jigsaw and can be as ornate as desired. The molding on the columns flanking the doorway arch can be made by utilizing purchased miniature-sized door casing moldings. It could also be produced by making several parallel kerf cuts with a thin saw blade, and then cut about $\frac{1}{32}$ inch deep to make the impression of the Italianate pillars.

The windows were fabricated from a Lexan plastic. Small sheets are available at most miniature shops, hobby stores, lumber yards, and hardware stores. These sheets are designed to be used as interior storm windows. The dentil trim that was used between the eave brackets is commercially available in assorted sizes, and adds to the nostalgic charm of the Victorian eave. The large corner blocks were made from $\frac{3}{4}$-inch lumber. Removable partitions were included to allow maximum utilization of the floor area for furniture arrangement. This miniature structure measures 18 inches deep by 28 inches wide by 31½ inches high. It has three stories and sufficient space for nine average-sized rooms. This style house has a flat roof, which eliminates the tedious task of shingling a large gable section.

The Cape Cod house shown in Fig. 9–3 is of the New England style salt box design. The siding utilized on this miniature house is individual strip siding. Another significant feature on this particular house is the false-front door. This permits maximum usage of the interior space for furniture arranging. The dormers break up an otherwise plain roof area.

The back of the Cape Cod house is shown in Fig. 9–4. This house was constructed with a completely open back to provide easy access for dec-

9–1
San Francisco rowhouse

Fig. 9–2
Hinged front panels

Fig. 9–3   Saltbox (front)

Fig. 9–4   Saltbox (back)

orating and arranging the selected furniture pieces. This house contains only four windows, so providing the necessary curtains or drapes to decorate the windows is not a major problem. The enclosed staircase in the Cape Cod provides additional wall space for hanging pictures and other artifacts. The separation of rooms is provided by the interior wall arrangement, which eliminates the need for interior doors and thus generates an open and airy atmosphere. This house measures 33 inches wide at the roof, 13 inches deep and 21 inches high to the roof ridge.

The English tudor shown in Fig. 9–5 has a coat of stucco that was obtained by utilizing sand textured paint. The study window is a custom-made unit, although this style can be purchased in approximately the same design. This house is considerably larger than the previously pictured Cape Cod. The English Tudor measures 50 inches long by 30 inches high by 20 inches deep. Movable partitions are used to allow for maximum room arrangement, to obtain the best possible display area for the miniature furniture. The back side of the English Tudor is shown in Fig. 9–6. Access to the attic area is provided by a cutout in the rear gable. The roof panels on either or both end gables could be hinged to provide additional storage area in the attic space.

The small miniature farmhouse shown in Fig. 9–7 was fabricated from cabinet grade birch plywood. It is elevated on a ¾-inch foundation to accent the porch. The rear of this house is shown in Fig. 9–8. The arrangement of the rooms permits interchanging of kitchen and living room on the first floor. It contains a large room on the second story which can be utilized as a combination bedroom/study. Access to the attic area is provided by a cutout in the roof and also a hinged roof section on the large gable end. This house is a smaller miniature house, measuring 25 inches wide by 20 inches deep by 23 inches high. Utilizing the cabinet grade plywood permits this house to be painted without the addition of siding. If a textured exterior is desired, use the miniature stucco mixture or sand textured paint.

The miniature house shown in Fig. 9–9 is another New England Cape Cod house. This particular house generates the maximum amount of room for the amount of material used. The house was constructed from ⅜-inch plywood and measures 13 inches deep by 26 inches long by 25 inches high at the roof ridge. The rear view of the slender Cape Cod is shown in Fig. 9–10. The partitions located on the first and second story are removable to allow for maximum room arrangement and easy access for decorating. The partition in the attic is also utilized as a roof support and is therefore glued in place. Access to the attic is provided by a cutout in the roof section. By completing this house with siding, shutters and a chimney the appearance is transformed into an attractive little cottage.

Fig. 9–5   English Tudor (front)

Fig. 9–6   English Tudor (back)

Fig. 9–7   Farmhouse (front)

Fig. 9–8   Farmhouse (back)

Fig. 9–9
Cape Cod (front)

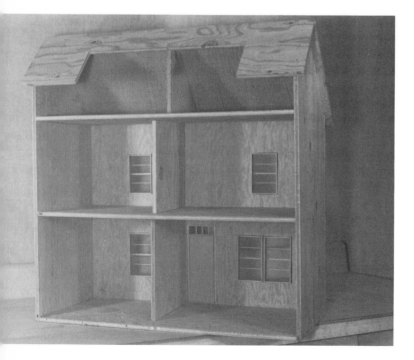

Fig. 9–10
Cape Cod (back)

Fig. 9–11
Chalet (front)

Fig. 9–12
Chalet (back)

The miniature house shown in Fig. 9–11 is a chalet styled house. It was constructed from ⅜-inch plywood and measures 26 inches wide by 13½ inches deep by 26½ inches high. The addition of a stucco finish, a balcony, and additional roof trim will transform it into a stylish chalet. Another finishing method would be to utilize batten strips, roof brackets and fishscale shingles on the gable end. A small chimney stack added to the roof would complete the exterior decoration. Paint any desired color. The windows are standard windows equipped with shutters. The back view of the chalet is shown in Fig. 9–12. This house has removable partitions to allow for ease of decorating and flexibility in furniture and room arrangement. Access is provided to the attic by a cutout in the gable. Note the roof support on the inside of the attic to strengthen the miniature structure.

Display Boxes

Individual miniature rooms are being produced as gracious repositories for the treasures of the miniature collector. These miniature boxes are being built in many different shapes and sizes, and when expertly finished can accent the decor of any room in your house.

There are many serious collectors of miniatures who prefer to display their more prized collectables in several individual rooms rather than in a complete dollhouse. This seems to permit more diversification in the number of furniture periods that one can concentrate on at the same time—each room being assigned a different style of furniture or a different time frame in history. French Provincial, King Louis XII and XIV, Queen Anne, Queen Victoria, Colonial American, Early American, Shaker, Italianate, Spanish Moroccan, Mexican adobe, and Japanese are among the many styles of furniture that individuals specialize in. Recently in the southwestern part of the United States, the Spanish-Mexican and Pueblo Indian cultures are having their influence on the miniature world. Expertly crafted pottery, basketry and wood carvings, predominately the Kachina dolls, are justly commanding high prices due to the high quality of the craftsmanship involved.

There are many sizes and styles of rooms available in ready made or kit form. They appear as Period rooms, display shops, vignette box and shadow boxes. The sizes of the various rooms range from 5 inches wide by 7 inches high and four inches deep, up to 24 inches wide and 12 inches high. Several small shadow boxes are shown in Fig. 9–13. These boxes measure 7 inches wide by 7 inches high by 3 inches deep, on the inside of the box. It not only is a shadow box for displaying miniatures, but also contains a top shelf for some additional miniature collectables.

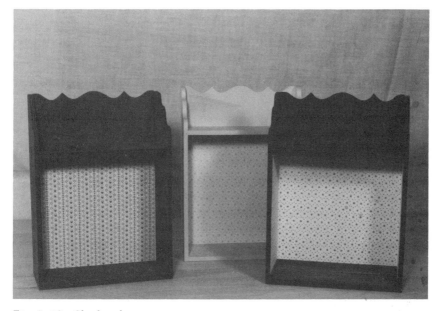

Fig. 9–13   Shadow boxes

Fig. 9–14   Decorated shadow box

Hooks can be added to the bottom side for holding keys, pot holders or small kitchen utensils. Figure 9–14 shows a decorated box.

This display box was fabricated from ¼-inch cabinet grade birch plywood. It can be stained or left natural. If other thicknesses are used, adjust the dimensions accordingly.

Materials List for Display Box

ITEM	DESCRIPTION	DIMENSIONS	QUANTITY
A	Back panel	¼ × 7 × 10	1
B	Side panel	¼ × 3¼ × 10¼	2
C	Shelves	¼ × 3 × 7	2

The pattern for the display box is shown in Fig. 9–15.

1. Cut the back panel, A, to the indicated dimensions, then cut pattern on top end as shown in Fig. 9–16 with a jig saw or sabre saw. Sand edges smooth. Apply a coat of stain; set aside to dry.

2. Cut the two side panels, B, to dimensions indicated, then cut pattern on top end of both panels to configuration shown in Fig. 9–17 with jigsaw or sabre saw. Sand edges smooth, then apply a coat of stain; set aside to dry.

3. Cut the two shelves, C, to dimension indicated. Sand edges smooth and apply a coat of stain; set aside to dry.

Fig. 9–15   Shadow box pattern pieces

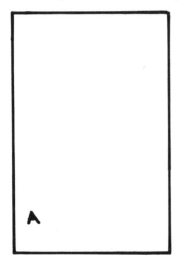

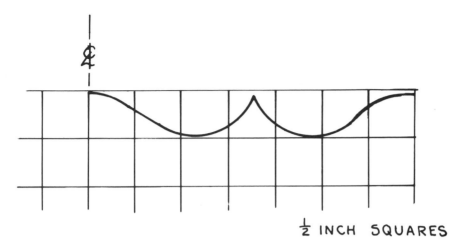

½ INCH SQUARES

Fig. 9–16   Box trim cuts

Fig. 9–17   Box trim cuts

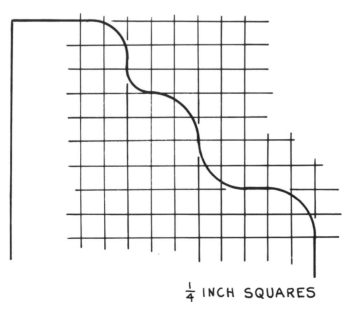

¼ INCH SQUARES

4. Attach one shelf, C, to the bottom edge of the back panel, A, flush with the corners. Then attach with glue and remove excess. Small brads can be used if desired but countersink nail heads.

5. Attach the two sides, B, to the sides of the back panel, A, flush with bottom shelf, C, and flush with back edge of back panel, with glue, removing excess.

3. If the display box is going to be wallpapered, do that at this time. The top shelf can be added later to conceal the cut edges of the wallpaper. Then add the top shelf, C, at desired height (recommend 7 inches) with glue, while maintaining squareness of shelf with side panels, B, and back panel, A. Remove excess glue with cloth.

4. Flooring and the baseboard trim can be added at this time if desired. This display box can be placed on bookcase shelves, table tops or it can be wall-mounted.

Antique Stores

It seems that each year more and more collectors of miniatures are increasing their collections by the addition of a quaint antique store. The store is one area in the miniature world where it is perfectly acceptable to mix vintage and style of furniture. In an antique store can be found elaborate displays of Shaker furniture alongside the bold Victorian style and the delicate style of Louis XIV. The beauty of the Queen Anne styled furniture can be enhanced by being displayed next to Colonial or primitive styled furniture. The variety of styles adds a special charm to the intrigue of the miniature world. Some collectors use their antique store as the warehouse for their dollhouses. A complete room arrangement can be replaced with a new and different style of furniture, and the displaced set can be then displayed in the Antique Shop. By utilizing the antique store, altering the room arrangements in conjunction with the doll house, a maximum variety of room arrangements can be obtained with a more limited amount of furniture and accessories. The antique store setting also allows an individual to specialize in one particular area of miniatures, such as painted china in a wide selection of patterns and styles.

The interesting display of collectables in the Antique Store shown in Figs. 9–18 and 9–19 belongs to the collection of Mrs. Harry Larson of St. Paul, Minnesota. The amount of intricate detail in each piece enhances the total display: the hand-painted china on the plate rails, the detail on the sconces, clocks and picture frames. The hand-carved back on the Victorian chair, the high back Windsor chair, indicates the dedication and craftsmanship of the builders. The handcrafted display case, with an inlaid teak wood floor, and custom-built staircase was a gift, built by her son. The display case has a removable front glass panel to permit easy

Fig. 9–18
Antique Store from the
collection of Mrs. Harry
Larson

Fig. 9–19
View of the store in 9–18
showing exterior of the case

access to the interior. This allows for the inevitable rearrangement of the miniature collectables, to obtain the most effective display of the total collection.

As newly acquired pieces are added to the display, a certain amount of rearranging is necessary to accommodate the latest addition. It may take several years to obtain a certain desired piece of furniture to eventually complete the collection and have the most desired furniture arrangement. But that is part of the intrigue of miniature collecting. The shop shown in Figs. 9–20 and 9–21 was designed as a dual-purpose building. It can be utilized as a two-story antique store, or with an antique store on the first story and the second story utilized as the owner's apartment. It was constructed with the front panel hinged to permit easy access to the building. The back panel can be temporarily attached with screws

Materials List for Antique Store

ITEM	DESCRIPTION	DIMENSIONS (IN INCHES)	QUANTITY
A	Side	$\frac{3}{8} \times 22 \times 11\frac{1}{2}$	2
B	Floor	$\frac{3}{8} \times 23 \times 11\frac{1}{2}$	3
C	Front Panel	$\frac{3}{8} \times 21\frac{1}{2} \times 23\frac{3}{4}$	1
D	Back Panel	$\frac{3}{8} \times 20\frac{1}{8} \times 23\frac{3}{4}$	1
E	Sidewalk	$\frac{3}{8} \times 3 \times 24$	1
F	Roof Cap	$\frac{1}{2} \times 1\frac{1}{4} \times 24\frac{1}{2}$	1
G	Eave Brackets	$\frac{1}{2} \times \frac{11}{16} \times 2\frac{1}{4}$	4
H	Front Corner Caps	$\frac{3}{32} \times \frac{3}{8} \times 19\frac{1}{4}$	2
I	Side Corner Caps	$\frac{3}{32} \times \frac{3}{8} \times 21\frac{1}{2}$	2
J	Window Sill	$\frac{1}{8} \times \frac{5}{16} \times 8\frac{3}{4}$	2
K	Vert. window Frame	$\frac{5}{32} \times \frac{5}{32} \times 5\frac{3}{4}$	8
L	Horizontal window frame	$\frac{5}{32} \times \frac{5}{32} \times 8$	6
M	Sign Board	$\frac{1}{8} \times 2\frac{1}{2} \times 14$	1
N	Base panel	$\frac{1}{8} \times 1 \times 2\frac{1}{4}$	4
O	Sign Letters	$\frac{1}{8} \times 1\frac{1}{2} \times 1\frac{3}{8}$	8
	Horizontal window casing	std $\frac{3}{8}$ molding $8\frac{1}{2}$	4
	Vert. window casing	std $\frac{3}{8}$ molding $5\frac{3}{4}$	8
	Window glass (plastic)	$\frac{1}{16} \times 5\frac{7}{8} \times 7\frac{7}{8}$	2
	Dentil trim	std $\frac{1}{2}$ wide $\times 22$	1
	Door frosted glass	std 3×7	1
	Victorian windows operating	std $2\frac{1}{2} \times 5$	3
	Door Knobs	std (purchased)	1 pr
	Hinges	std $\frac{3}{4}$ inch butt type	1 pr

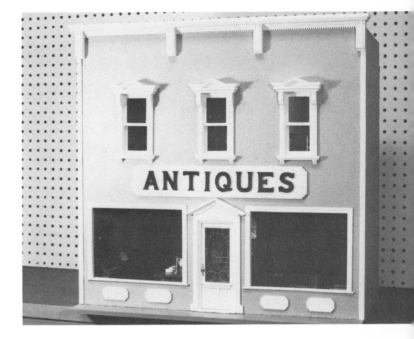

Fig. 9–20
Antique shop (front)

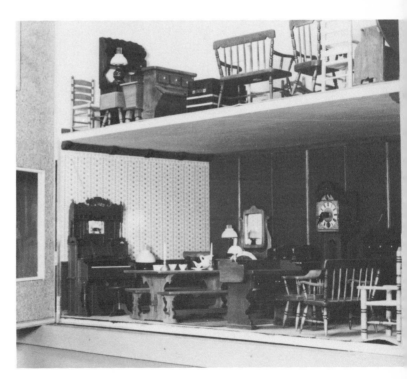

Fig. 9–21
Antique (back)

if access to the back side is desirable (or if expansion is considered) or it can be permanently attached with glue and nails.

The lower section of the inside back wall was paneled with wainscoting, and the upper portion of the wall was covered with flocked gift wrapping ribbon between strips of wainscot cap trim. This unit was built from ⅜-inch plywood; two coats of sand textured paint were applied to the exterior to obtain the stucco effect. The Victorian styled windows and the frosted glass front door add another dimension to its fascination. This store front and sides can also be fabricated from particle board to obtain the appearance of a stucco finish.

Assembly

Pattern for antique store is shown in Fig. 9–22.

1. Cut two sides, A, to dimensions with a table saw. Sand edges lightly.

2. Cut three floors, B, to dimensions indicated with a table saw, then sand edges lightly.

3. Cut the front panel, C, to the pattern shown in Fig. 9–23. Use a framing square to establish the locations for the openings of the windows and door. Then drill starter holes with an electric drill for a sabre saw to cut the openings. Sand edges lightly.

4. Cut back panel, D, to dimensions indicated with a table saw. Sand edges lightly.

5. Cut sidewalk, E, to dimensions on a table saw, then sand lightly.

6. Cut roof cap, F, from a ½-inch thick piece of pine to dimensions indicated, then using a router and bead profile cutter, produce the bead configuration shown in Fig. 9–24 on the front and two sides of the board. Sand edges lightly.

7. Cut four eave brackets, G, to proper length, then cut two kerf cuts with table saw or hand saw, then radius one end, as shown in Fig. 9–25. Complete all four brackets in this manner.

8. Cut two window sills, J, to length indicated, then modify both ends of each piece as shown in Fig. 9–26, using table saw or jigsaw. Sand saw cut edges lightly.

9. Cut one sign board, M, to dimensions indicated, then cut the four corners as shown in Fig. 9–27 with a jigsaw. Sand edges and front, lightly.

10. Cut four base panels, N, to dimensions indicated, then cut corners as shown in Fig. 9–28 with a jigsaw. Sand lightly.

11. The patterns for the individual sign letters, O, are shown in Fig. 9–29. Trace letter on ⅛-inch stock material with tracing paper and carbon paper. Then proceed to cut individual letters with a jigsaw.

12. Cut the required two panels of window glass (plastic) to proper size.

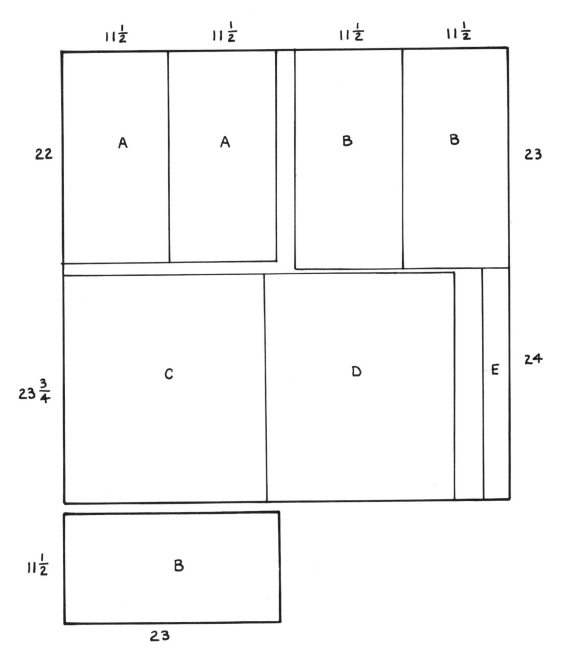

Fig. 9–22   Pattern pieces for antique shop

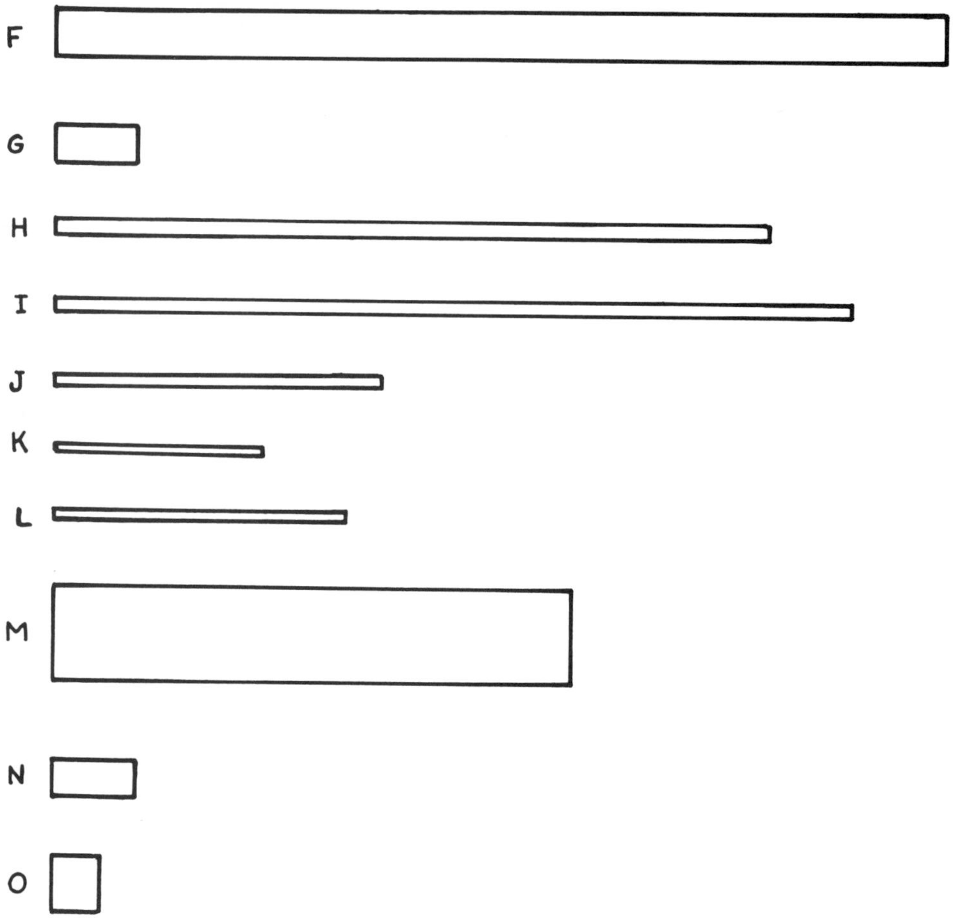

F

G

H

I

J

K

L

M

N

O

Fig. 9–22 (continued)

13. Cut remaining pieces to proper thickness and width but leave the cutting of the length until the assembly, to adjust for any variations and assure a snug fit.

14. Obtain the necessary hardware and trim and then proceed to assembly.

Assembly

1. Paint the front panel, C, any desired color; several coats may be required so use a quick drying variety. If a stucco texture is desired, use either the standard miniature paint designed for stucco finish or sand texture paint. Paint the following items a flat white: roof cap, F; eave

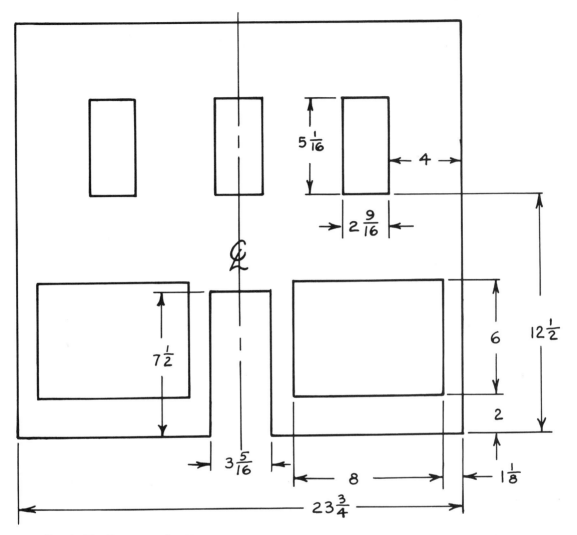

Fig. 9–23 Front panel pattern

Fig. 9–24
Roof cap pattern

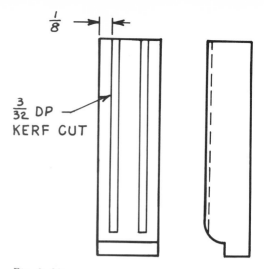

$\frac{1}{8}$

$\frac{3}{32}$ DP
KERF CUT

Fig. 9–25
Eave bracket pattern

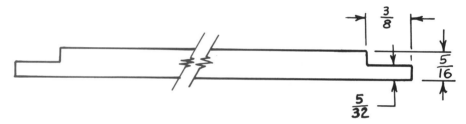

$\frac{3}{8}$

$\frac{5}{16}$

$\frac{5}{32}$

Fig. 9–26   Windowsill pattern

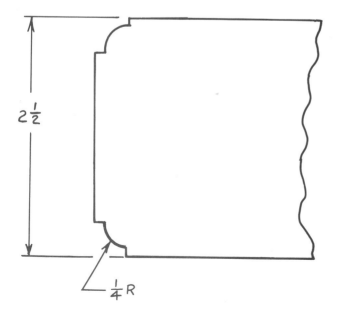

$2\frac{1}{2}$

$\frac{1}{4}$ R

Fig. 9–27
Sign board pattern

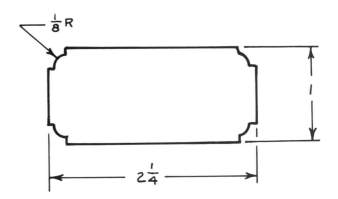

Fig. 9–28
Base panel pattern

Fig. 9–29 Letter patterns

brackets, G; front corner caps, H; side corner caps, I; window sill, J; vertical window frame, K; horizontal window frame, L; sign board, M; base panels, N; window casings, dentil trim, door and Victorian windows.

Paint the Sign letters, O, a flat black. Paint sidewalk, E, with a flat gray (concrete color). Set components aside to dry.

2. Assemble the three floors, B, between the two sides, A, at a 9½-inch floor-to-ceiling height, for both stories, with glue and nails. Apply glue clamps until glue has dried, after removing excess glue. At this point it would be advisable to decorate the interior walls and floors with wallpaper and paint if desired, including back panel, D.

3. Back panel, D, can be permanently attached with glue and nails or temporarily attached with screws for ease of removing.

4. Attach the window sills, J, to the front side with glue.

5. Insert the two glass windows behind the window sill, J, with a small amount of glue on the edges.

6. Cut the required six horizontal window frames, L; place one each behind the glass at the window sill level, then place one on each side of the glass at the top; install with glue flush to edge.

7. Next cut the vertical window frames, K, to obtain a snug fit. Place one in front of the glass and one behind the glass on both edges of each window. Attach in place with glue and flush with the edge.

8. Cut vertical window casing at 45 degrees on one end, fit other end flush with window sill and also flush with vertical window frame. Apply in place on both sides of two windows. Attach in place with glue and remove excess.

9. Cut horizontal window casing at 45 degrees on both ends to fit between the vertical window casing members at the top, both inside and outside, and at the bottom on the inside only. Attach in place with glue, removing any excess glue.

10. Next attach the roof cap, F, equally spaced from right to left and flush with the back of the panel, with glue and nails. Remove any excess glue.

11. Install the side corner caps, I, flush against the roof cap, F, and flush with front edge of store front, with glue and nails. Remove any excess glue.

12. Install two of the eave brackets, G, flush with edge of corner cap, I, and roof cap, F, with glue. Equally space the remaining eave brackets between the window openings and attach with glue.

13. Next attach the front corner caps, H, flush with edge of side corner cap, I, and against bottom of eave bracket, G, with glue, and remove excess.

14. Cut the strip of dentil trim to size to fit between the eave brackets in three places, attach in place with glue.

15. Attach door knobs to both sides of door. Then glue door assembly in place, removing excess glue. (If door comes with casing material for the interior, install that at this time.)

16. Next attach the sidewalk, E, to the bottom of store front panel, C, with nails and glue, flush with each side and flush with back of the panel. Remove excess glue.

17. Install the Victorian windows in the openings with glue. (If windows are provided with additional casing material, install it on the interior at this time.)

18. Place the completed front panel assembly next to the floor assembly and attach hinges to side of choice, either right or left.

19. Lay the sign board, M, on a flat surface and position sign letters, equally spaced from side to side and top to bottom. When in desired position, glue in place. Add weight to hold in place until glue has dried. When dry, position on store front panel equally spaced from side to side and between windows and door gable, then attach with glue and remove excess.

20. Next position two base panels, N, equally spaced below each store window; attach with glue and remove excess.

House Kits

The selection of architectural styles of miniature house kits has tripled in the last few years. Anyone desiring to obtain a specific style of house, in kit form, also has a choice from a wide range of sizes. A score of manufacturers are producing houses that vary in size from a small single-room house up to and beyond a stately twelve-room mansion. Three and four-story houses are the rule rather than the exception. The styles available include the Cape Cod, New England Saltbox, Colonial, Williamsburg Colonial, Southern Colonial, Southern Plantation, Federal, Georgian, Queen Anne, Victorian, Farmhouses, Contemporary, English Tudor, Cottage and Chalet. Not to mention the Log Cabins, greenhouses and a variety of specialty shops.

If a specific room arrangement is desired and not available, there are an untold number of craftspeople who specialize in custom-built miniature houses. These people are located throughout the country, from east coast to west coast. One of the houses available by mail order is the Victorian mansion shown in Fig. 9–30, from The Dollhouse Factory. You can write for their catalog, which has a range of houses available in

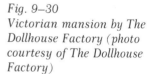

*Fig. 9–30
Victorian mansion by The
Dollhouse Factory (photo
courtesy of The Dollhouse
Factory)*

various sizes and styles. The address is given at the end of Chapter 5. The house kits provide all the individual parts, cut to size and ready to assemble. The kits are available in various types of lumber. The better-quality kits are produced from a fine grade of birch plywood. This is probably the best grade of plywood available and would be highly recommended, providing the desired room arrangement can be obtained.

The instruction sheets that are provided with most dollhouse kits are detailed sufficiently to eliminate any potential problems. The manufacturers of the better house kits produce the individual piece parts to the necessary shape and size so adjustments are very minor if required at all. Other houses are built to a lower standard and are manufactured from Phillipine mahogany plywood. This type of plywood is brittle, and splinters easily; it is difficult, if not impossible, to sand the edges to obtain a smooth finish. Therefore, houses built with this plywood are to be avoided. Between these two extremes are many varieties of quality designed houses that are completely acceptable for the miniature collector. Variations in style, size and price range are considerable, so decide what is desirable and then shop around.

Ready-Made Houses

Many miniature retail shops have a wide selection of ready-made houses available, in addition to the many styles in kit form. Some of these miniature shops have styles and designs produced solely for their shop by local craftspeople. In most instances the people who produce these houses do so in a very limited quantity. That is one reason for such a diverse selection of miniature house styles among the individual miniature shops.

In other miniature specialty stores, the owner is the builder responsible for the display of houses. One example of this is the collection of dollhouses found at Debbie's Dollhouse located in Minneapolis, Minnesota. The craftsmen in this case are a father-and-son team, Jim and Dan Humphrey. Some houses are built as a team; others are built by the individual. A few examples of their work can be found in Figs. 9–31 through 9–34. Some of their finished miniature houses have appeared in TV commercials, which by itself speaks highly of their work. They maintain a large selection of miniature houses throughout the year, varying in style and size to accommodate discerning miniature enthusiasts.

Custom-Built Miniature Houses

In practically every state there are a number of craftspeople who devote their time exclusively to building custom-made miniature houses. A custom-made house can be a historical replica or a specific architectural style house not quite so famous. The craftsperson builds a specific house for a specific patron. Producing a limited number of these each year, the craftsperson often concentrates on a specific architectural style and incorporates as much of the minute detail as is humanly possible. This specialization, in one style of house, produces some of the finest replicas of historical monuments which exist. There are many well-qualified craftspeople who have generated such a tremendous demand for their work that they have a waiting list for the next two or three years.

Specialty Shops

Many miniature collectors have changed their emphasis from doll houses to specialty shops. A shop may consist of a custom-built store or a single

Fig. 9–31   Dollhouse, built by Jim and Dan Humphrey

Fig. 9–32   Dollhouse, built by Jim and Dan Humphrey

Fig. 9–33   Dollhouse, built by Jim and Dan Humphrey

Fig. 9–34   Dollhouse, built by Jim and Dan Humphrey

room, in addition to their regular collection in a miniature house. This specialty shop may be a bakery with showcases and wire display racks filled with decorated cakes, pies, rolls and trays of cookies. It may be a plant shop with complete floral arrangements, potted plants and hanging baskets complete with miniature macrame. Other types of shops might include a cafe, a sporting goods store, an art dealer, a bookstore, a country general store, a boutique shop, or a western tack shop. The specialty shop variation is limited only by the imagination of the builder or designer.

One specialty shop is shown in Fig. 9–35. This miniature shop is a woodworking shop called the Wood Mill. The interior view shown in Fig. 9–36 shows the various aspects of a wood shop, with carved duck decoys and Kachina dolls, picture framing material, sconces on the walls, chairs with carved backs, benches, stools and a sundry of other pieces.

The miniature shop is basically a rectangular box, with the addition of siding and trim to the facade. The individual letters that are attached to the front comprise the sign board for the structure. The basic structure can be altered to fit any type of specialty shop that is desired.

This shop was fabricated from ⅜-inch plywood. The pattern for the individual components is shown in Fig. 9–37.

Materials List for Specialty Shop

ITEM	DESCRIPTION	DIMENSIONS (IN INCHES)	QUANTITY
A	Floor	⅜ × 7⅛ × 12	1
B	Sides	⅜ × 7½ × 9¾	2
C	Roof	⅜ × 7⅛ × 12	1
D	Front	⅜ × 12 × 12¾	1
E	Back	⅜ × 9¾ × 12	1
F	Sidewalk	⅜ × 2¾ × 12¾	1
G	Top trim	⅛ × ½ × 13	2
H	Front trim	⅛ × ½ × 11⅜	2
I	Side trim	⅛ × ½ × 12	2
J	Window	1/16 × 5¼ × 5½	1
K	Horizontal window frame	⅛ × 5/32 × 5 9/16	3
L	Vertical window front	⅛ × 5/32 × 5 1/16	4
M	Window Sill	⅛ × ⅜ × 6 9/16	1
N	Window trim vertical	1/16 × ½ × 5 9/16	2
O	window trim horizontal	1/16 × ½ × 6 5/16	1
P	Door (purchased)	3 × 7	1
Q	Siding (Purchased)	as required	
R	Butt hinges, ¾-inch (Purchased)		1 pr

Fig. 9–35   Wood Mill specialty shop

Fig. 9–36   Wood Mill interior

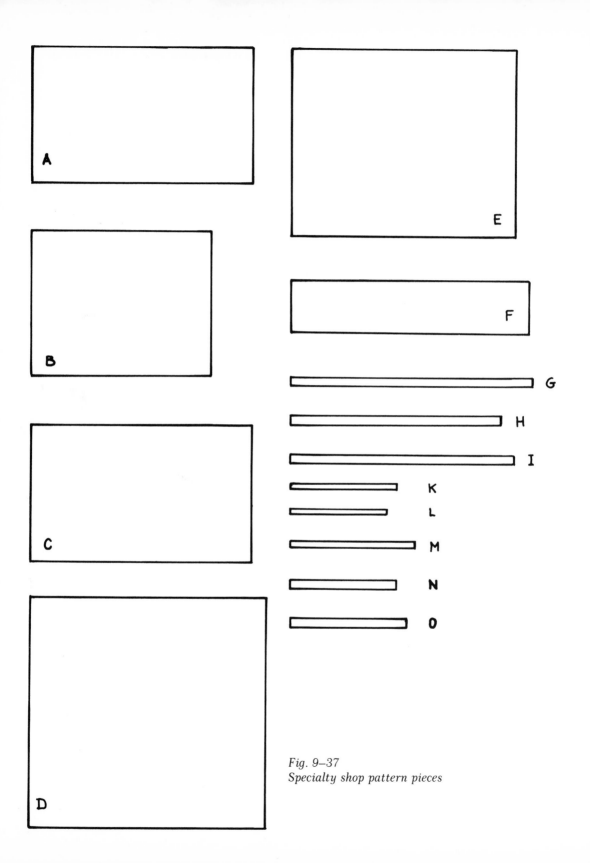

Fig. 9–37
Specialty shop pattern pieces

Cutting Pieces

1. Cut the pattern for the floor, A, to the dimensions indicated. Sand edges lightly to remove any splinters.

2. Cut the pattern for the two side panels, B, to the dimensions indicated. Sand sawcut edges lightly.

3. Cut the pattern for the roof section, C, to the dimensions indicated. Sand sawcut edges lightly.

4. Cut the pattern for the front, D, to the dimensions indicated and to the pattern shown in Fig. 9–38. To cut the window and door openings, first drill ⅜-inch starter holes with an electric drill, then cut out openings with a sabre saw to the required dimensions.

5. Cut the pattern for the back panel, E, to the dimensions indicated. Sand edges lightly.

6. Cut the pattern for the sidewalk, F, to dimensions indicated and sand edges lightly.

7. Cut two pieces of the top trim, G, to the dimensions indicated from

Fig. 9–38   Shop front pattern

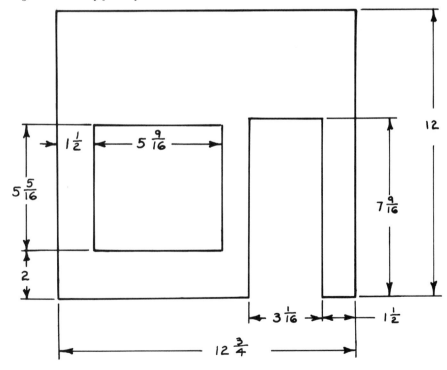

⅛-inch stock of basswood or pine. Sand edges lightly to remove any sawcut marks.

8. Cut two pieces of the front trim, H, to the dimensions indicated from ⅛-inch stock of basswood or pine. Sand edges lightly to remove any sawcut marks.

9. Cut two pieces of the side trim, I, to the dimensions indicated from ⅛-inch stock of basswood or pine. Sand edges lightly to remove any sawcut marks.

10. Cut the window, J, to the dimensions indicated from a plastic sheet, either Lexan or Plexiglas.

11. Cut three pieces of the horizontal window frame, K, to the dimensions indicated. Sand edges lightly.

12. Cut four pieces of the vertical window frame, L, to the dimensions indicated. Sand edges lightly.

13. Cut the windowsill, M, to the pattern shown in Fig. 9–39, and the dimensions indicated. Sand edges lightly.

14. Cut the two pieces of the vertical window trim, N, to the dimensions indicated from a ¹⁄₁₆-inch basswood or pine strip. Then miter one end of 45 degrees to match corner of mating piece. This part can be fabricated from standard exterior window or door casing also.

15. Cut the horizontal window cap trim, O, to the dimensions indicated from a ¹⁄₁₆-inch thick basswood or pine strip. Then miter both ends to match the vertical window trim parts, N, at the corners.

16. The remaining components, door, siding and butt hinges, items P, Q and R, will be added to the structure after the unit has been assembled.

Assembly

1. Assemble the two sides, B, to the foor, A, with glue and nails. Position the sides flush with the front of the floor. Remove any excess glue.

Fig. 9–39   Shop windowsill pattern

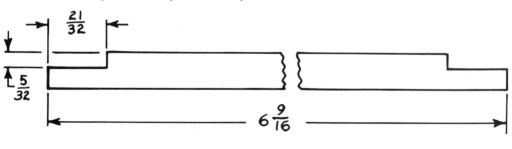

2. Assemble the roof, C, to the sides, B, at the top edge and flush with the front. Attach in place with glue and nails.

At this point in the assembly, it may be desirable to decorate the interior of the miniature shop before proceeding with the completion of the basic structure.

3. Assemble the back, E, to the sides, B, and flush with the roof and the floor, items, C and A. Remove excess glue.

4. To the inside of the window opening, assemble two horizontal window frames, K, with glue and flush to the inside of the store front, D; remove any excess glue.

5. Assemble two vertical window frames, L, flush to the inside of the front, D, and flush against the two horizontal window frames, K. Remove any excess glue.

6. The window section, item J, can be inserted into the window opening without glue, if desired, against the previously installed window frame.

7. Place the windowsill, M, at the bottom of the window opening and attach in place with glue. Remove any excess glue.

8. Next install the remaining horizontal window frame, K, to the top portion of the window opening and flush with the front surface of the store front, D, with glue and remove excess.

9. Install the two remaining vertical window frames, L, between the horizontal window frame, K, and the windowsill, M, with glue. Remove excess glue.

10. Install the two sections of the vertical window trim, N, with glue and flush against the window sill, M. Remove excess glue. Hold trim in place with weight or glue clamps.

11. Attach the section of the horizontal window trim, O, between the two vertical trim pieces, N, with glue. Remove excess glue, and hold in place with weights or clamps.

12. Attach the two top trim sections, G, to the store front D. Place one top trim section flat on the top of the front, D, and also to overlap the other trim section on the forward side of the wall, with glue. Hold in place with spring clamps until glue has dried.

13. Attach the two side trim pieces, I, flush with the front edge of the store front, D and flush with the underside of the top trim, G, with glue. Remove excess glue. Hold trim in place with clamps until glue dries.

14. Attach the two front trim pieces, H, one on each side of the front, D, flush with the side trim, I and also flush with the top trim G, with glue. Remove excess glue and use spring clamps to hold trim in place until the glue dries.

15. Paint the section of sidewalk, F, with a light colored gray paint to

resemble a concrete walk. When the paint has dried, attach to the bottom of the store front, D, with glue and nails, flush with the inside and flush with each side.

16. Cut standard siding, Q, to the required dimensions to fit the entire store front D, but do not glue in place. Paint siding desired color. Then place the cut pieces of siding on a flat surface and apply weights until the paint has dried.

17. While the paint on the siding is drying, apply a coat of paint to the store front trim and the window trim, then set aside to dry.

18. Paint the door, P, the desired color and set aside to dry. The door will be installed after the siding has been attached.

19. When the paint on the siding is dry, attach the cut siding, Q, to the store front, D, with glue. Then apply weights to the siding to prevent the siding from curling until the glue drys.

20. Install the painted door, P, with glue. Place a weight on the front of the door to hold in position until the glue has dried.

21. The letters for the name of the type of store selected can be any desired style or thickness. The height of the letters shown in the photograph are ¾ inch. A signboard could also be added and the individual letters than attached to the signboard. Various styles of lettering could be used to accent the selected name of the shop, including Old English, Roman block or script style.

22. Attach the two butt hinges, R, to the store front, D, and the desired side wall, B, depending upon the direction of opening desired. Use an awl or an ice pick to locate screw holes.

23. To complete the exterior of the side walls, B, either paint or apply clapboard siding.

INDEX

INDEX